NUTS AND BOLTS IN SCHOOL ADMINISTRATION

John W. Stallings

D. Lloyd Nelson

371.2
St/8n

Good administration is more than sound theory and facts. In addition to many other necessary things, the excellent administrator must know how to organize and administer at 8:00 a.m. tomorrow in the office.

We spend much time in books and classes in administration considering philosophy, psychological theories, and sociological principles in the abstract to the point that practical application, in many cases, is lost.

It is true that consistent, long-term, superior administration depends upon research, solid theory, and worthy principles. But this knowledge is of little value unless it can be practiced effectively. We know that most administrators are dismissed not because they know too little, but because they cannot apply what they do know with the people involved.

Statements from the general public or from employees within an organization such as "he/she is a good administrator" or "he/she doesn't know the first thing about administration" indicate judgments based largely on day-to-day operational situations. They are not derived from in-depth analysis of the philosophical considerations in the issue. Such perceptions do indicate the importance to the administrator of functioning effectively in these numerous instances.

This book is designed, in part, to meet this need. We call the points presented "Nuts and Bolts" because they are the devices that will hold administrative behavior together. Admittedly, the points are situational and should not be used in every circumstance; some may be even contradictory. Thus, knowing when and how to use each point will still depend upon your judgment.

Our hope for this book is that it will stimulate your thinking, sharpen your powers of operation, contribute to the enjoyment of your job, and help you in your administrative position. We will be pleased if it does a part of any one of these things.

JWS
DLN

January 1978

ABOUT THE AUTHORS

John W. Stallings has a distinguished career as a professional educational adminis- trator. He has been a teacher at elementary, junior high, high school, and university levels; he has been an elementary principal and a high school principal; he has been an assistant superintendent and a superintendent; and he is presently a professor of educational administration at the University of Southern California.

Dr. Stallings has served as Interim Dean, School of Education at USC, and is presently Chairman, Department of Educational Adminis- tration and Supervision. He is a popular teacher--his graduate students are highly complimentary about his teaching and research abilities, but they love him most for his warm, human qualities.

Dr. Stallings has an impressive list of research publications. His written works the last two or three years have dealt mainly with Declining Enrollments and Auditing School District Financial Transactions. Dr. Stallings has served as chairman for more than 100 doctoral research studies in educational admin- istration and has served as chairman of the USC faculty doctoral committee for the School of Education.

ABOUT THE AUTHORS

D. Lloyd Nelson is recognized as an outstanding educational administrator, especially in school business administration. He has served as a teacher, principal, and superintendent. For 27 years, Dr. Nelson served as a professor of educational administration, specializing in school finance and business administration at the University of Southern California. While in this position, he directed over 200 doctoral research studies, served as advisor to hundreds of graduate students, and was a competent teacher to thousands. He has worked with countless school boards, superintendents, and other school administrators. He has served as consultant to school districts, intermediate units, employee organizations, and state departments of education. He served, also, as Chairman, Department of Educational Administration and Supervision.

Dr. Nelson was selected to be the Distinguished Professor of Educational Administration (Melbo Chair), School of Education, University of Southern California for the academic years 1977-1978 and 1978-1979.

Dr. Nelson has two major textbooks among his numerous publications. The first is a history textbook adopted by the State of California for eight years entitled Yesterday, the Foundation of Today. The second text is School Business Administration for which Dr. Nelson is the senior author.

Both authors have been active in numerous
administrative organizations for educators.
They have effected change by their leadership
in these professional organizations. The
authors' greatest contributions, though, have
been the positive changes in the very lives
of thousands of graduate students who have come
under their influence and counsel. This book,
Nuts and Bolts in School Administration, reflects the quality of leadership which both
authors have made to the field of educational
administration.

TABLE OF CONTENTS

Page

II. TECHNIQUES OF LEADERSHIP 59

PART I

PRACTICING THE ART OF ADMINISTRATION

NO ONE SAID IT WOULD BE EASY

There should be some mathematical
equation that shows worthwhile results as
a function of hard work and effort on the
part of the administrator. Certainly the
effective leader is not one who quits looking for work after he has a job. You must
expect to work a little harder, a little
longer, and a little better than those
workers whom you supervise.

The difficulty of the work will be perceived by you in relation to how well you like
the work. If you enjoy your work, it will not
be hard even though it is demanding, time
consuming, and complicated. If you don't
like your work, even the simplest tasks will
be chores that will weigh you down.

But a word of caution: Don't become
a "work-a-holic." Don't become so addicted
to the job that you neglect family, friends,
and other important aspects of living. Enjoy
your work, but enjoy other things, also.
Some administrators we know become so buried
in their work that they are social bores,
narrow human beings, and completely frustra-
ted when forced to retire.

- - -

A robot would make a poor administrator.
If all the ideas given by the authors in this
book are followed meticulously, you will be
a poor robot and a poor administrator. There
are exceptions to nearly every good general
rule.

It is better not to spend most of your time on yesterday's mistakes, or putting out today's fires, but spend most of your time and energy planning for tomorrow.

BE PREPARED

Never appear to make a presentation or
conduct a meeting unprepared. Be sure to do
your homework. Have the loose ends tied.
In many situations it is the job of the school
administrator to have answers so proper decisions can be made. You waste the time of
important people if you don't have the data
required.

The PTA executive board will resent it
if the principal gets them to a meeting to
discuss buying some playground equipment if
the principal does not know: (1) the approxi-
mate cost or whether the school district will
accept the gift; (2) where it would fit on
the school grounds; (3) who could supply the
equipment and how soon; (4) whether the equipment is desired by the students and faculty.
And much more.

The Board of Education expects the administration to be informed on a revised program
of studies being proposed.

The school administrator speaking to a
taxpayer's group about a school election had
better have facts and figures.

And don't feel just because you've spent
hours preparing data that you must use it all.
Don't feed an entire load of hay if the cows
aren't hungry. It is just as easy to lose a
point by talking it to death as it is by not
knowing enough to say about it.

Be informed, be prepared, have your homework done. Then use this preparation wisely.

5

Hmmm. . . We need a meeting of the Building
Committee to decide if the Fire Department
should be called, and then . . . .

That there should be participation in decision making is not entirely true always. If you discover the school building is on fire, you sound the fire alarm, phone the Fire Department, and take other necessary procedures. You don't stop to have participation in your decision making by members of the faculty, classified staff, pupils, and the PTA president. You act!

On the other hand, full participation should have taken place prior to the fire as to what procedure would be used should a fire take place. Custodians should participate in decision making regarding brooms and mops they will use. The Doctoral Committee, School of Education, at a major university consists of five professors and two graduate students. At each meeting many decisions are made, particularly regarding special student petitions. The votes of the two students count the same as those of the professors and often their two votes may decide an issue. Yet, students alone don't make the decision, but they do "participate."

Teachers should be "in on" decisions regarding textbooks and supplies, their salaries, working conditions, etc., but they should not make the final decision. In a representative democracy, the school board hopefully does allow for full participation of all concerned.

Often it is best to say, "Let's put that idea on the back burner, not forget it, but have it close at hand for subsequent consideration as things develop."

7

Sure would be nice if there were a few
more people to delegate some of this
responsibility to!

An elementary school principal missed eleven days of work because of illness. Upon returning to work he found his desk stacked with paper--maintenance work orders, supplies requisitions, attendance reports, and dozens of other similar documents.

The principal went through the paperwork and divided it into three stacks: one, items he wanted to decide; two, items he wanted to review but not be held up for his approval; and three, items he had no need to see at all.

To his surprise there were only two documents in the first stack--a teacher's report on a third grade girl and a parent's letter inquiring about how spelling was taught. The second and third stacks shared about equally the balance of the items.

Most administrators would find about the same if they truthfully analyzed their jobs. At least 75 percent of the decisions they make could be made better by other people. About half of these the administrator should know about for information and communication; the other half the administrator doesn't even need to review. Only about 25 percent of the decisions should be his to make. And by delegating the others, the administrator can do a much better job on that 25 percent.

Remember when you give away responsibility, delegate also the authority to get the job done and then be prepared to support the outcome.

"What and how" means to tell what is to be done but then let the individual decide how to do it. Like all good points, this can be carried to an extreme. You certainly would not tell a cafeteria employee to wash the dishes without first teaching how to operate the dishwashing machine and telling about safety and health factors to be observed.

But to tell a professional employee to keep graded test papers in the first drawer of her desk and ungraded papers in the third drawer is out of place.

A school board should tell by policy what level of transportation they want for the district, but the board should not figure out the bus routes.

A school system operates by delegation. A board or a superintendent that refuses to delegate becomes a bottleneck to effective leadership. A superintendent or board can no more handle everything in a district than a principal can teach all the classes in the school. The principal must delegate to teachers; the superintendent must delegate to principals; and boards must delegate to the superintendent.

One of the unexpected and often pleasant surprises from not telling an employee *HOW* is that the job will be accomplished more effectively the employee's way than by the way you would have recommended.

BE ADAPTABLE

An administrator moving through a busy
work day will possibly be involved in a
different type of activity every 15 minutes.
In one activity you may need to be a whirling
dervish, in another a passive listener. In
another situation you may be alone and in the
next be with a group of 300 people or more.
You may go from being the main attraction to
being nobody in the same hour.

These many changing roles call for
adaptability on the part of the administrator; the ability to change gears. You need
to recognize the personal speed limit in
each activity and race your motor or slow
down as needed. Use your third eye: If
your intuitive sense tells you to behave in
a certain way, listen to it.

Be adaptable. At times supply booster
shots of adrenalin, at times apply the brakes.
Learn to enjoy the variety of activities
associated with your work.

But above all develop some interests
outside your job that give you pleasure;
learn to enjoy spending time by yourself
doing things you like. This refueling
technique will give you the extra energy
you need to be successful in the multiple
activities of your work.

- - -

Have fun with your life!

11

Nothing is more important to the school administrator than his relationship to other people. Studies indicate that 85 percent of all people dismissed were released because of lack of human skills. This is true for all types of employment even those fields of work not generally considered to need good personal relations.

You can relate to another person by understanding his situation, his problems, and his successes. Empathy means caring, identifying with a person, and being sincere about it.

A person can sense when you don't really care about him. He knows if your interest is faked and false. When he detects insincerity in you, he will suspect you have other negative qualities such as lying and dishonesty.

A pushy, self-centered person is not empathetic. He is too selfish to care about others and is very seldom liked. You will walk into his office six feet tall and come out feeling four feet shorter.

You must condition yourself to be sincerely interested in other people--to be empathetic. Practicing this will make you not only a better administrator but a better human being.

- - -

Knowing what motivates individuals is a key to obtaining better performance.

MAKE THE LITTLE THINGS COUNT

What kindergarten or first grade teacher has not had her job described as making the little things count? The admonition here though is to college presidents, district superintendents, principals, and all other school administrators.

A president of a major university sent a beautiful gold embossed invitation to a prominent, prospective lady donor. The invitation was to the Ambassador's Circle-- a prestigious group of wealthy contributors to the university. This lady graciously rejected the invitation and although she had been favoring that particular university, she selected another one to which she donated a quarter of a million dollars. The lady's name had been misspelled on the invitation.

Automobile manufacturers know the value of the little things, the finishing touches on new cars. The best salesmen have the little important techniques perfected to an art form. The school administrator, also, must remember how much difference little things make. They either count for you or against you and most school administrators need all the help they can get!

- - -

Make it a special point to remember the names of everyone you work with and see often--custodians, secretaries, wives of colleagues, and not just board members or those you feel are important.

13

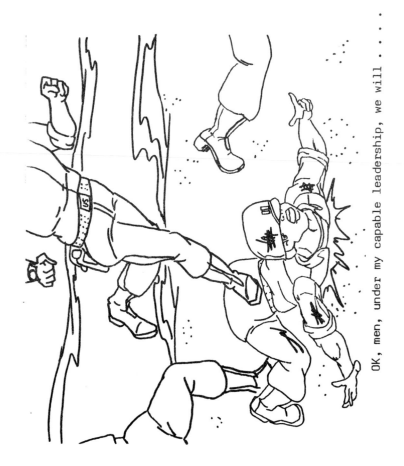

OK, men, under my capable leadership, we will . . . . . .

LEAD OR GET OUT OF THE WAY

An administrator by definition is the leader, the person out front, the one pointing the direction. The leader inspires teamwork, maintains high morale, and helps others grow on the job. When two or more people are working together, one of them must be the leader to get the job done.

There is the vacuum principle in administration which says that if the administrator doesn't administer, then someone else does--someone fills the void. Several semi-humorous slogans emphasize this point including, "I must hurry and catch up with my troops, I am their leader."

There are times when the administrator should not lead and in those cases he should get out of the way and let someone else administer. The elementary principal should turn over to the chairman of the teacher's social committee the decision about where and how to have the annual faculty picnic. The PTA should organize the scrap paper drive and the cafeteria manager can plan the lunch menus. So, leadership does not mean that all the decisions must be made by the administrator or that no decisions are to be made by him. It does mean that, overall, an administrator should lead or get out of the way.

- - -

Optimism is contagious. Is your cup half full or half empty?

GOSH! I have to make a decision!

16

MAKE DECISIONS

You are employed to make decisions--then make them! Make them and if eight out of ten are right you are doing fine. Too many weak administrators adopt the concept that if they just do nothing, maybe the problem will go away. It is the doctrine of laissez faire, let a sleeping dog lie, why stir up trouble, do nothing and the problem will solve itself.

On the other hand, if the warehouseman has always stored mimeograph paper on the top shelf by climbing a ladder, the schools won't close if a hydraulic forklift is not pur- chased before noon. Snap decisions can make you look foolish by frequent retractions and costly mistakes. To operate on a snap deci- sion basis as a matter of routine leads to making decisions without all the facts, violating democratic procedures, and loss of staff support.

But too often fact gathering, testing the situation, committee formation and such are just substitutes for making decisions.

In most cases it's not too great a calamity whether the meeting is set for 7:00 or 7:30. Often it is not a big deal in case of cloudy weather whether a principal decides to have a rainy day schedule or not just so he decides something so the teachers, bus drivers, custodians, and cafeteria workers can plan sensibly for the rest of the day. Many decisions are neither right nor wrong. Someone (you) just needs to decide something so others can proceed. So make decisions!

17

AVOID THINKING OF A PERSON AS YOU KNEW

HIM FIVE YEARS AGO

The entire concept of education is that people can change, yet a common mistake is classifying a person as he used to be.

Remember seeing a friend for the first time in several years and observing how striking the physical changes were? And have you noticed how you tend to overlook the gradual changes in people you associate with daily?

Now translate this into professional growth of your associates. The green, young account clerk of five years ago is now a competent, experienced accountant; the beginning teacher is now a reading specialist; and the new elementary principal now has his doctorate and is ready for central office administration.

Therefore, when writing recommendations or when thinking of promotions be sure to update your opinions of people. Don't think of people as they were five years ago.

Unfortunately, most of us do a better job of keeping current on negative progress of individuals than we do on positive progress of individuals. Although it is possible to change either toward or away from improvement, we tend to remember that Frank has become an alcoholic but we forget that Paula has her master's degree.

A superintendent of schools met some opposition from the school board when he recommended a high school teacher for promotion to counselor. It finally came out that two of the board members remembered the teacher when he started teaching several years before. He had discipline problems and although he had overcome this early setback and had been extremely successful in the last five years of teaching, the board was still classifying him on what he had been years before.

The world's religions believe people can change; many wives have molded husbands; and now it's time for school administrators to evaluate people as they are today and not as they were five years ago.

THOSE COLD MEMOS

Don't administer by memos. Use the personal touch when feasible. There are times "you want it in writing," or to save time it's the right thing to do, but doing nearly all of your communication by use of memos is to be avoided. They are impersonal, cold, permit people to read between the lines, and necessitate another memo if some point is not clear. On the other hand, for "information" items or "yes" answers, they are highly desirable.

When gross negligence has been exercised, when insubordination has occurred, or when you are misquoted and embarrassed, it is appropriate to write a memo eating someone out or telling him off. This is good therapy. However, hold the memo for 24 hours and then throw it away! Or at least you will feel more like softening it for a more intelligent and less emotional response.

No, I don't think me or my boys could fix your car,
but could you hang on until I find somebody who
can?

FIFTY-ONE PERCENT OF SMART IS KNOWING
WHAT YOU'RE DUMB AT

A young business manager proved he was smart on at least two occasions by admitting he was dumb. In the first situation the school district was incurring excessive telephone bills. The business manager confessed he did not know about telephone equipment but that he could identify a consultant who could give advice on the district's telephone system.

An independent specialist in telephone operations, maintenance, design, and equipment was employed and he studied the district's problem for two days ($500 cost) and recommended one piece of equipment ($2,000 cost) that saved the district about $30,000 in telephone bills the first year.

The second circumstance arose when the district began preparing its annual transportation report. This document was the district's certification of expenses to the state for reimbursement of transportation costs. The school district's business manager again obtained the services of a consultant, a specialist in transportation. The specialist charged $200 for one day's work in the district, but the district qualified for $10,000 more in transportation aid than they ever had before.

Whatever your position in administration you're not expected to know everything about all things. Instead of bluffing your way along or repeating last year's mistakes, it is far better to admit that you're dumb. Then be smart enough to employ someone for the short term who knows what he's doing.

SAYING NO

If you are going to say "No" to a person who feels deeply about the matter, do it in person and not by telephone or letter.

It is all right to say "Yes" almost any way--by memo, letter, telephone or carrier pigeon. This favorable answer will not alienate the receiver no matter if it is impersonal. But a "No" on a sensitive or important issue should be done face to face.

Every time you say "No" you cannot and should not do it personally. Requisitions disapproved because budget allocations are exhausted do not require personal attention unless you wish to propose an alternate course of action to be followed. An educational field trip denied for the present because two buses are broken down and no other bus is available is another illustration of a routine "No."

An assistant superintendent of instruction went to the junior high school to deny the English Department's proposed curriculum revisions. As he sat down with the teachers and started discussing the plans, the teachers immediately said that they weren't happy with their proposals and would like to study them some more. The assistant superintendent offered to provide an outside consultant to help the teachers develop the new English program. Everybody went away happy whereas if the assistant superintendent had sent a memo to the school saying "No" to the English proposal, the teachers would have felt affronted and unappreciated for their efforts to improve the junior high English program.

You will find that by saying "No" in
person you very often never have to say it
at all; at least when you do it can be softened
and explained--and accepted without hard
feelings.

Remember the importance of timing.
Many right moves can be spoiled if not timed
correctly.

It is the wrong time to present proposals
for reduction in athletic expenditures three
days before the home team plays in the champion-
ship game. It is the wrong time for the
superintendent to request a raise in salary
from the board just after he has presented a
monthly financial report that is unbalanced
and in the red.

It is very difficult to develop any set
rules about when is the right time, but a sense
of good timing must be developed by the school
administrator.

Perhaps the rocket launches into outer
space illustrate the importance of timing.
The scientists compute the present and future
positions of the planets; they determine
trajectory of space vehicle as affected by
weight, thrust, gravitational attraction; they
determine optimum times for launching the new
space probe.

School administrators need the same
skills in timing the launching of new educational probes. Good timing is important.

THE EXCEPTIONS

Policies are made to be broken; rules are to be circumvented; procedures are to be changed--for the exceptional situations. And those exceptions in most cases are humanistic ones--ones where grave injustice would be done by following the "books."

It was a wise high school principal of a rather small (500 pupil) school who permitted an 86 year old man to enroll in regular day classes. This elderly gentleman wanted to graduate from high school before he died. He was readily accepted by the students and became a great favorite on the campus. Fortunately, the old gentleman realized his dream because he did graduate at the end of the school year. And he did die before the next year was over. Can you imagine the attitude of the community and the pupils if the principal had enforced the school policy of no pupil over 21 years of age in day school? The principal would have lost all respect.

And there was no demand from others that they be granted the same privilege. School administrators are generally too fearful to deviate from procedure because they assume a flood will cascade through the crack. What is needed is a greater faith in people that they, too, will understand the need to deviate-- to make the exception.

- - -

Know what your problem is first before you start solving it. We often formulate solutions to false perceptions rather than to real problems.

24

BE A MEMBER OF THE TEAM

One of the most difficult things to do in some situations is to support the boss, especially if you know he's wrong. As a professional you have every right to present your side, to try to influence a different decision, to support your point of view. But despite your best efforts the boss says do it my way--and he is the boss.

Your job then is to get on board--not to fuss and grumble and complain. Do it the boss's way and, who knows, it may even be better than you thought. Most things can be accomplished in a variety of ways.

There are situations when the above advice breaks down. One of these is when you are directed to proceed illegally--when you are instructed to break the law. As an example, a superintendent might direct the business manager to buy the superintendent a new car from a local dealer without following the state laws on school purchasing. In these illegal cases the administrator should respectfully refuse to act and suggest the difference be arbitrated by the next higher authority--in this example, the board of education.

In other situations, the instances of differences between you and the boss may be so frequent and of such magnitude that you should simply resign.

But these are extreme situations and not representative of most conditions. In the majority of cases, being a member of the team is the best and proper role for the school administrator.

I am NOT promoting you to the new position because you
are such a FINE employee!

SUCCESS IN ONE POSITION SHOULD NOT

BE A PENALTY TOWARD PROMOTION

"Things are going so great at Washington School that I hate to think of taking Jim out to head the elementary curriculum department."

Have you ever been in a personnel selection committee when an administrator made a remark like that? Unfortunately too often instead of rewarding a person for outstanding performance, the person is ruled out of promotion--because he is doing so well where he is.

Remember also that a new position, or different assignment, helps an employee in the renewal process. It give him new motivation, stimulation, creates afresh the excitement of discovery.

A word of caution: Just because an employee was outstanding at one position does not guarantee that he will be outstanding in another. There is always the Peter Principle. And any farmer knows you can't plant the same crop in any type soil. People, too, have certain abilities that suit them for particular positions.

Despite this it's best to look first at proven performers when choosing for advanced positions and don't penalize the successful person.

- - -

Henry Ford is quoted as saying that you can't build up a reputation on what you are going to do.

MANAGE BY OBJECTIVES

The most important element of management by objectives is that the employee and his supervisor agree on what the employee is to accomplish.

It is not unusual for the superintendent to go along doing what he thinks should be done and the school board fumes and burns because certain things they think important go undone. It is very important that they get together and lay out specifically what is to be accomplished and when.

Measurable objectives should be developed for board, superintendent, principals, and all other school administrators. The performance of each administrator should be evaluated in terms of achieving those objectives.

It is not necessary to try to prepare objectives for all things an administrator does. An objective should be thought of like a test item on a final examination: It is a sample. It represents a spectrum of possibilities.

Objectives provide a viable, valid procedure for management of people and organizations by school administrators.

- - -

In solving a problem, get the whole picture first and then see if the pieces fit the whole. Don't start with the pieces to develop the whole.

BE SURE TO VISIT THE CUSTODIAN

Visit the custodian not to check up on him and evaluate his work but very simply to become his friend. It is well worth the time to have a cup of coffee occasionally with the custodian in his storeroom. Usually he has been around the school much longer than most of the certificated people and he has a wealth of practical knowledge about operating the school.

Don't try to pump the custodian about the teachers or about parents. It's true that he probably knows many community people who you will not likely get to know. And it's true that he has opinions about the teacher's abilities drawn from marks on the walls, scratched desks, and papers on the floor. But don't expect the custodian to do your job for you--and it is your job to evaluate staff and to meet with parents.

The custodian should know what kind of program he is sweeping up after. Frequent, friendly visits by the school administrator will help educate the custodian in the educational program area. The custodian will become a lot more understanding and helpful when he understands why it is important for the third grade teacher to have those messy finger paints.

Visit the custodian--because he is a person as you are a person. He is a member of your team. His role is as important in many ways as yours. If you have all the friends you need and want, forget the custodians, but be sure your personnel file is up to date.

29

ANONYMOUS LETTERS AND CALLS

As a school administrator there is only one appropriate way to officially handle anonymous letters and telephone calls. That is to ignore them. The letters should be thrown in the trash and the calls forgotten.

But the advice is not 100 percent effective. The exceptions are those anonymous calls or letters with threats involved. The threat of danger to lives or property even though anonymous must be dealt with. This includes the involvement of the proper agencies such as police, fire department, and bomb squad. The school administrator should carefully record details of the communication: time, exact wording of message, distinguishing characteristics, etc.

The advice to ignore the contacts applies to the majority of anonymous communications since most of them deal with the personal lives of employees or gossip about someone connected with the school. These messages are usually true, at least in part. It is the manner of gaining the evidence that makes it advisable to disregard them. Under no circumstances should the administrator place anonymous letters or messages in the employee's personnel file.

Nor should the administrator call the employee in and inform him that he has received an anonymous letter or call about the employee. If you plan to ignore the communication, the very act of talking to the employee about it means you are not officially ignoring the message.

The anonymous telephone caller who wishes
to complain about a teacher or tell you about
gambling by the football coach should be
informed by the school administrator: "My name
is Ole Tegner. I am principal of Washington
School. Unless you give me your name, I plan
to hang up the phone. Anytime in the future
when you want to call and identify yourself, I
will be pleased to discuss any matter involving
our school with you." Then, if the caller
doesn't identify himself, hang up.

CREATING DEBTS

An ancient truth identifies the probab-
ility of losing a friend by loaning him money.
The financial debt creates a chasm in relation-
ships.

The point here is that a wedge is also
driven between human beings by creating personal obligations. It is bad administrative
practice to become deeply obligated to a
person or to have a person deeply obligated
to you.

When an administrator becomes deeply in
debt to a person or to several people, he
restricts his ability for future actions. A
good principal can hardly suspend the son of
a local judge if the judge has recently "fixed"
a traffic ticket for the school administrator.
The business manager will have difficulty
prohibiting the maintenance man from using the
school's paint sprayer to paint the maintenance-
man's house if the business manager borrowed
the school's hedge trimmer.

From the other side, if a person is
deeply obligated to you, he will begin to

31

feel inferior. He perceives his personal
worth devalued in your estimation. He will
avoid associating with you.

Notice that the admonition here is
against deep obligation. Human beings, which
includes most school administrators, must
exchange small favors. Common courtesies
and thoughtfulness always are appropriate.
It's when these become excessive that you
create debts.

SELECTIVE BLINDNESS

The best teachers know what to see and
correct but more importantly what to overlook
and ignore. The pupils involved in many
instances are better able to resolve situations and arrive at equitable answers if left
alone than with adult intervention.

This is equally true with adults in
schools in relation to administrators. The
principal and other supervisors must use
selective blindness. Some things must simply
be overlooked.

If left to their own devices, the custodian and the cafeteria manager will probably
resolve the problem of getting the folding
lunch tables in place in time for serving lunch
to the pupils. Whereas, if the school principal steps in, he will likely alienate one or
both parties.

The Citizens Advisory Committee can work
out differences on how to conduct a school
paper drive or what booths to have at the
Halloween Carnival. No need for the administrator to lose friends and support by taking
sides.

The real problem, of course, and the leadership quality that separates the excellent from the average administrator is the ability to select when to be blind.

TELL AN INQUIRER ONLY WHAT

HE WANTS TO KNOW

When asked a question, give a direct answer. If more detail is wanted, it will no doubt be requested. When detailed explanations and an elaborate defense are given, a sense of doubt or guilt is generated.

Remember the old story about the young boy who raced into the house and yelled: "Mommy, where did I come from?" She thought the time had come so she sat him down and explained in detail about the birds and bees. "Any more questions?" she asked.

"No," he replied, "the new kid down the block said he came from Oklahoma."

Too often the superintendent is asked a question by a board member and an answer of "Yes" or "No" or "I don't know" is all that is wanted. In answering such a question if you make a speech, time is wasted and you get the reputation of talking too much and monopolizing the meetings.

Also, when responding to inquiries, it is better not to over-color or exaggerate the answers. If two board members disagreed sharply at a board meeting, they did not have a fight; and if the architect's building plans require a change order, the plans are not necessarily ridiculous, impossible, disgraceful, and worthless.

Do not oversell. When an idea, plan, or point is sold, quit talking.

AVOID DUALISM

A school district central office staff of 18 women was having trouble. A survey team that was called in to investigate found that six of the women were working for more than one boss. This was leading to confusion of assignments, time priority, and misunderstandings. Each employee should have only one immediate supervisor at any one time. Dualism of bosses should be avoided.

Another form of dualism exists when two administrators report to the Board of Education; usually one is responsible for financial affairs and one for the educational programs. This is bad organization and should be avoided. The line and staff organizational pattern is recommended for schools. In this pattern only one administrator, the superintendent, reports to the board and an assistant superintendent for business reports to the superintendent.

A third type of dualism that is usually bad is the assignment of responsibility of a task to two people at the same time. For example, don't have two people developing independently a duty schedule for teachers at a school or two people working separately on buying 30 typewriters for the high school business department. You may end up with no teachers on duty in the cafeteria and too many teachers on the playground. The business department may also get 60 typewriters instead of 30.

Dualism, then, can exist in assignments and/or organization. Wherever it exists, it should be removed for the sake of better school administration.

35

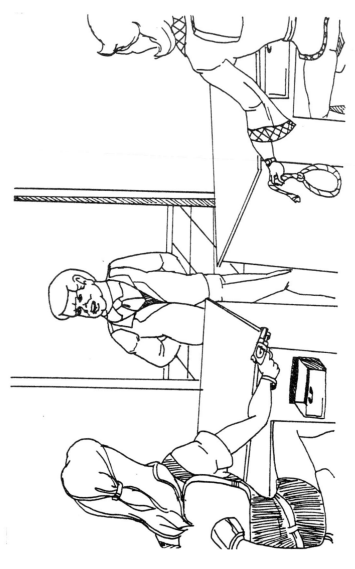

I feel I should warn you that I am going to recommend coffee breaks be cut from 20 to 15 minutes.

ADVANCE WARNING

When time permits, tell those who will probably object to board or administrative action, what your recommendation will be on the matter, in advance.

If you are going to recommend to the school board that coffee breaks for secretaries be reduced from 20 minutes to 15 minutes, let the secretaries know well in advance. True, it may give them a chance to oppose you, get organized, and develop opposition you would not have had. On the other hand, they will always respect you for being a square shooter. And if your recommendation is not sound enough to withstand opposition, it should not be enacted.

A university school survey team working with districts on problems of declining enrollments was always careful to make sure that parents and teachers of schools being recommended for closure were told well in advance. These parents would circulate petitions to keep their schools open and make numerous public statements. But none of these statements ever accused the consultant team of being unfair or dishonest. The recommendations were well publicized and never was an attempt made to sneak an action through the school board.

As a by-product, the school administrator will probably do a better job of gathering data and developing reasons for recommendations if he knows he is likely to be challenged. The topic will be thought through better.

Any school administrator would rather have the image of honesty and fair dealing rather than an image of being sneaky and an

under-the-table operator. Warning your
opposition ahead of time will help build this
favorable image.

PAY PREVAILING WAGES

        The school administrator who tries to
operate an organization by paying low wages
is headed for trouble. It is far better to
pay adequate wages and have fewer people than
to pay lower wages and have more people.

        If wages fall too far below averages,
then the morale and spirit of the staff suffer.
Commitment of the people to the organization
diminishes and productivity drops.

        In school settings there are usually
finite amounts of funds available for salaries.
The more these fixed amounts are divided, the
lower the salary per person and there can be
a correlation between quality of service and
level of salary.

        Ask any parent to choose between having
his child in an average teacher's room with
fewer pupils or in an excellent teacher's room
with more children. Which would be the room
selected?

        Wouldn't you resist sending a school
busload of children off on a trip with a
driver recruited at the cheapest wages possible?
Or would you rather have fewer trips with a
capable, well-paid driver?

        Paying prevailing wages to fewer employees
is a better choice than having more employees
working for cheaper salaries.

ESTABLISH AND OBSERVE

CHANNELS OF COMMUNICATION

Communication within channels applies
to a variety of situations. One of them is
transacting business at the right place and
time, not on the street corner or in someone's
house. The superintendent should avoid plug-
ging on a point listed on the next board agenda
to a board member at a social affair or at
the Rotary Club.

The superintendent should not by-pass the
high school principal and supervise the football
coach.

Proper channels of communication should
be established by board policies, organizational
charts, and job descriptions. There is always
need in any organization for communication not
only up and down but across the various levels.
Sharing of information need not stay in established channels but communication designated
to direct the affairs of the organization should
stay in channels.

It is easy for the board to by-pass the
superintendent on occasions, particularly at
times when the business manager or other administrators have information the board wants.
Board members should not request a report of
vandalism losses from the business manager
nor should the board request a report on third
grade reading from the assistant superintendent
of instruction.

The board has only one direct employee--
the superintendent. It's best to keep communications in proper channels.

He'll be good for the football team, eh?
Well, send him in; I'll have a look at him.

CHECK THE CANDIDATES PERSONALLY

The good school administrator is never
satisfied to stop when screening candidates
for a position with written references. Nor
is the addition of a personal interview
sufficient to gather enough data on a candidate. It is essential that personal contacts
be made and discussions held with people knowl-
edgeable about the candidate.

An hour spent by telephone or in talking
in person may save days and weeks of time
later. Most supervisors will be much more
candid in speaking than in writing.

The selection process, then, should be
to use the written personnel files for rough
screening; the interview for narrowing the
field to three or four finalists; and the
follow-up personal contacts to identify the
top candidate. Be sure to include that last
step--checking the candidate personally--for
each position for which you are responsible.

CHOOSE THE PERSON FOR THE POSITION

Each organization has certain functions
that are performed by people in different
positions. An administrator must guard against
changing these organizational functions to fit
people instead of choosing people to fill the
needs of the organization.

A very capable job candidate may have
exceptional skills in public relations, be a
beautiful blond and a friend of the school
board president. This candidate should be
rejected if what the school district needs

in the position is an elementary curriculum specialist to develop a primary reading program.

It's sort of like being in a food cafeteria line. The cool, crisp salads; the hot, steamy entrees; and the rich, creamy desserts all look good. But if you have only 50¢ and are dying of thirst, you should stick to the drinks to fulfill your need.

There are many tempting candidates for positions with a wide variety of specialties to offer. Be sure to select the person for the position; don't change the position to fit the person.

K.I.S.S.

Much of the school administrator's job is to explain programs to various publics, describe situations in multi-media, and instruct subordinates. It is relatively easy given the specialized jargon of education to confound and confuse. This added to the natural inclination for obfuscation of many administrators tends to result in too many, too long, too obtuse oral and written reports. What is needed is stricter adherence to the K.I.S.S. idea: <u>K</u>eep <u>I</u>t <u>S</u>hort and <u>S</u>imple.

In developing a proposal for a year-round school, the administrator will undoubtedly compile pages and pages of research data, procedural guides, and experiential information. A review of related literature will be produced, visitations to similar programs in other schools will be conducted, and proposed application will be made to the administrator's own setting.

42

Then comes the K.I.S.S.--the difficult
task of shortening and simplifying the year-
round program to one or two pages for presenting to the parents, or for presenting to
the School Board or Citizens Advisory
Committee.

The report should begin with the recommendation stated very clearly. Then the report
should have two or three paragraphs describing
the program, a short paragraph giving three or
four major reasons for the program, a short
paragraph stating two or three major reasons why
not, and then a conclusion with a short explanation of how the program could be applied.

Again, this total report and all other
similar presentations by the school administrators should be kept short and simple,
not over two pages and preferably one.

THE TOP BANANA STILL IS IN

TOUCH WITH THE BUNCH

Have you known a rising young administrator who thought the way to the top was by
stepping on his co-workers? Or the fellow
who, when promoted, promptly forgot his lowly
former friends?

This type of person is headed for the
"elevator experience" in administration. He
may rise to the top but without the help and
support of the other levels of people in the
organization, he will end up again at the
bottom.

Some administrators have to learn this
the hard way and the second time up they

43

maintain contacts and build strong vertical support. They become top bananas but they still keep in touch with the bunch.

. . . and I would like to thank all those who have brought me to where I am today.

44

A wise superintendent developed with his administrative staff of 25 people (including principals, assistant principals, other leadership personnel) the concept that each of them would develop a specialty. Each person could choose his own area to develop expertise--elementary physical education, primary grade reading, pre-school education, family life education, or whatever. Professional library materials or resource personnel were provided for training.

Then each administrator was available to serve the other schools of the district upon invitation by the principal. The school district had 25 specialists to help improve the educational programs.

Each administrator was an expert and utilization of his competence contributed to his feeling of esteem. The specialist gained prestige that increased his level of importance and made him a better administrator.

You can become a specialist in one field, also. Select an area and attend a university class, develop a reading list, join a committee of your professional organization, select appropriate conference meetings to attend, and talk with authorities in the field. You will be a more valuable employee for the district and your own feelings of competence and self-worth will be increased.

- - -

The country folks in the midwest have a good piece of advice: "Dig your well before you are thirsty."

Hmmmpph. . . I wonder if anything new is going on.

KEEP UP TO DATE

It is important, of course, to keep
current on educational matters if you are a
school administrator. You must run fast just
to keep even in methods of instruction,
curriculum revisions, and school business
trends.

But it is equally as important to keep
up to date on the social customs, personal
habits, and beliefs of the young people in
your schools.

How many school level administrators
got caught fighting beards, hair length, and
short skirts? And this was long after they
were accepted modes of appearance by most
general publics.

A district level school administrator
loses touch if he doesn't spend time in the
schools where the young people are. Contemp-
orary music is also helpful. Current movies
tend to be responsive to youth. Some comic
strips do a good job of pinpointing differences
between youth and "the establishment."

Now please don't over-apply this point so
that you as an administrator find yourself
following every passing fancy and frill.
Don't change the dress code to sanction "topless"
just because a topless bar opened downtown. But
do change your policy and permit pregnant teen-
age girls to attend school. These young
expectant mothers are no longer outcasts from
society.

47

Keeping up to date with youth is not as closely related to age as you might expect. Some school administrators are still thinking young the day they retire while some young administrators are atrophied in the job after the first year. Keeping up to date is more mental than chronological.

WHEN TRAPPED IN YOUR OFFICE

Upon occasion the talkative, obnoxious visitor stays and stays long after any business matters have been handled. You are trapped in your school office and your broadest hints are ignored. Now is the time to put your pre-planned escape plan into action.

You should develop your own plan. One superintendent of schools had his secretary, upon buzzer cue, come in and say, "You remember, Dr. Jones, you have that very important meeting and you are already late."

Another superintendent had a much more direct philosophy. He felt that a person so unthoughtful as to stay and infringe upon his time deserved little consideration. So he would rise and remark, "We have concluded our business, Mrs. Smith, and I have a very busy schedule. Please excuse me."

In some cases the staying habits of a visitor are known and the general rules can be made clear before the conference starts, "You have a 15-minute appointment, Mrs. Smith, from 10:00 to 10:15."

The school administrator can pick up the telephone and buzz his secretary and say,

"Miss Miller, will you please tell my next appointment that I'll be with him in just a minute? We are about finished with our business in here."

Whatever the device, it is a good idea to have a plan worked out so you can get out of the trap in your own office.

I'd like to stay and talk longer, Mister Ness, but I really must go!

It's time to initiate the back-up plan, Roscoe: Let's get the heck OUTTA here!

HAVE A BACK-UP PLAN

Pilots have an alternate landing field
in case the primary site is fogged in; firemen
require an escape route when the elevators are
blocked; teachers know all children won't
learn reading by one method; and school administrators, also, must have a back-up plan.

When the voters reject a revenue bond
proposal, the administrator better have a
plan for housing pupils in some way other than
new classrooms. When the PTA turns thumbs
down on the principal's idea of having a cake
sale to raise money for meals for needy pupils,
have an alternate proposal for raising money.

The voters are not against housing pupils
nor is the PTA against meals for needy pupils.
It is the method of accomplishing these aims
that are vetoed. Therefore, devise alternate
methods and have them in reserve. Don't get
caught without an escape route.

Having a back-up plan doesn't mean that
the administrator must develop two answers for
every problem. In a lot of cases the contingency plan is a referral back to the administrator. For example, if the board of education
is not satisfied with the candidate being
recommended by the superintendent for a vice
principal's position, the superintendent should
request that the board refer the appointment
back for another recommendation at a subsequent meeting.

- - -

Think twice--and say nothing.

BE A PART OF THE COMMUNITY

One of the best junior high school principals we've ever known organized a horse show at
her school and rode in three events. The community loved her because at least one family out
of every three had horses.

Living in the community, associating
with parents in various activities, and getting
to know and be known by local citizens can be
argued pro and con. In our opinion, the pros
far outweigh the cons.

Being a part of the community means
associating with noneducators. Get to know the
hairdresser, the bank president, the editor,
and the postmaster. You will discover that
people only expect school administrators to be
human beings--not gods. The days when a school
administrator was perceived as a saint are gone.
By the same token, if you're too much a sinner
you are doomed. Bad debts, drunken brawls, or
immoral behavior make for a short administrative tenure. But if your desire is to live
like that, you probably can't live far enough
away from the community.

Live where you work and be a part of the
community. And in return you will really get
to know your community and how the people
feel about the schools.

— — —

*When the newspaper misquotes you, as a general
rule, do nothing.*

I DARE YOU TO STEP ACROSS THIS LINE

A superintendent of schools in a small district told the school board they could choose between him and a new school bus. If the board insisted upon buying a new bus he was resigning. To start the next school year, the district had both a new bus and a new superintendent.

Another superintendent in a large urban conservative school district fought for and was dismissed because of his pet project-- sex education for elementary school boys and girls.

There are situations where the administrator may want to fight and die for a principle. But in 99 percent of the cases you are better advised to remember that you don't own the schools--the people do. Your job is to make the best recommendations you can, give the best advice you can, and then do it the other way, if directed to do so.

Of course, you are within your rights to refuse to perform illegal acts. And in other cases you may want to keep a written record of why you did it the boss's way.

But the major point to remember is that when you draw the line and dare your boss to step across it, chances are almost sure that he will.

- - -

An administrator does not own his desk, the buildings, or the school buses. An exhibition of proprietary interest is resented by citizens and employees.

53

Tell you what: I'll let YOU go first!

54

YOU DON'T HAVE TO BE FIRST

School administrators who try to make a
reputation for themselves by being the first to
implement a new idea seldom last very long in
the district. Being a pioneer is hazardous.
The time lag between the introduction of a new
idea in education and its acceptance by the
public is generally several years. Forcing
the acceptance of an educational concept on
the public before they are ready involves
great risk on the part of the administrator
as well as the creation of numerous opponents.

Pioneers aren't as successful as you
imagine, anyway. Columbus died in disgrace,
thinking he was a failure. Mark Twain went
deeply into debt investing in new schemes
that the nation wasn't ready for. Being first
can mean being first to make a bad mistake.

So it is much better, especially if you
are a new administrator, to use tried and true
methods and programs and leave the experimen-
tation until you have established yourself.
Then you can afford the luxury of being first
to try something new and controversial. You
don't have to be first; you can profit from
the mistakes of others.

- - -

*Don't spread yourself "too thin." It
is better to select the things you must be
sure to handle right and do them right rather
than getting mixed up in so many activities
you don't do anything right.*

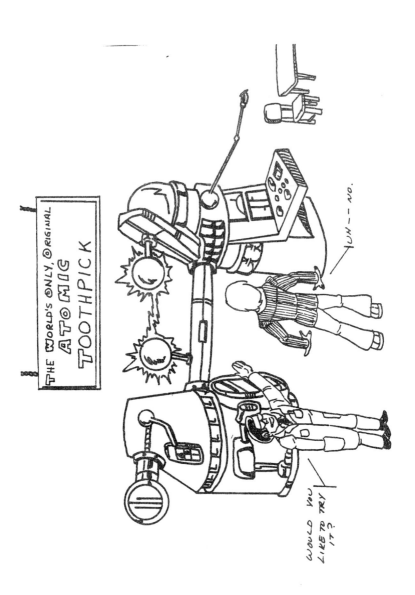

When you are given a new position with
new responsibilities, it is generally accompanied with new worries. Among those worries
is the uncertainty caused by unfamiliar
conditions: unknown people to associate with;
strange reports to process; unusual procedures
to follow; and new circumstances to become
familiar with. You should expect more than
normal feelings of anxiety and greater incidence
of mistakes in this situation.

Lesser administrators in these conditions weaken in will, become insecure and buckle
under the new responsibilities. The capable
administrator, meanwhile, will work harder than
normal, seek help from others, laugh at himself, and succeed in learning the ropes of the
new job without becoming unraveled.

Just remember that your boss and others
believe you can do the job or you would not
have been appointed. The Peter Principle
does not apply universally and in your case
you have much further to go before reaching
your level of capability. Many people before
you have done the job you are tackling or,
at least, jobs similar to it. And you can do
it, too.

- - -

Anything worth doing is worth doing badly--
as opposed to waiting for perfection before
trying something. We are not on earth ALL
that long for all conditions to be perfect.

You are on your own, Boys; but I DO have some helpful suggestions!

PART II

TECHNIQUES OF LEADERSHIP

I convinced the boss today to follow my
advice. You know, he's a pretty smart guy!

Nothing makes an employee feel better than to bring a problem to the "boss" and be asked, "What do you suggest?" When the employee gives his advice and it is accepted, the boss can reply by saying, "Thanks. That is good thinking. Let's do it your way." Then the employee has told himself what to do instead of being told; he will take more interest in doing it, and he can tell his spouse that night how smart he is.

This or any other procedure mentioned in this book, if used in every situation, will become trite and so recognized by the staff. It will be resented and thus become a poor way of working. However, use this technique frequently with the right people, but not to absurdity. There are some situations where you and you alone must decide and it is even inappropriate to ask for advice.

In teaching a class composed of military personnel, one of the authors recommended this procedure and was really "jumped on" by the class members. They argued that "the superior is paid more than we are to make the decision-- he ought to make it--and also such a technique would indicate a weakness on his part."

Even with these possible weaknesses (at least in a military setting), "What do you suggest?" is an appropriate and recommended technique in many instances for school administrators.

IS SONG OF PRAISE WORTH

MORE THAN MONEY?

Most studies indicate that the primary concern of teachers is not the low salary received, but desires for a feeling of belongingness, security, being appreciated and wanted, and an opportunity for partici- pation in decision making. After such factors as these, better salaries are then listed by teachers in morale surveys. Of course during serious salary negotiations in a district, salaries would be listed as first.

Sincere praise of individuals, when deserved, goes a long way in improving feel- ings of security, being appreciated, being wanted, and improving belongingness. Insin- cere praise and that given when not really deserved is considered as backslapping, as political maneuvering and as an insult to intelligence.

We all work better through love than through fear. A little deserved praise is appreciated by even the cynic. It can help make up for inadequate salaries paid by a poor district or for other unhappy situations. Use praise wisely, discretely, and with proper timing. It doesn't have to be conversational praise. It can be a one sentence long-hand note of "thank you for the great job you did yesterday."

- - -

Some of the most productive time an adminis- trator can spend is in devising ways to give others credit who did their jobs well.

62

Stop and think for a minute. How many
times in the last week have you complimented
someone? If the answer is less than twice a
day, you are missing the boat in improving
morale. Positive reinforcement is an accepted
and sound principle of modern psychology.

Of course the better answer is sincere
praise and money--no one despises either!

TODAY'S ORCHID

The superintendent-principal of a high
school district with one school of 1,000
pupils developed the Orchid Concept which is
worthy of use by others in small districts.

She used a daily bulletin tacked on the
bulletin board in her outer office. The
bulletin also served as a "check-in sheet"
for all employees to initial, and thus it was
read by all employees. Near the bulletin was
a paper orchid and under it read "Today's
Orchid Goes to _____." Then the reason for
the "award" was given.

The citation could be to Julie James
for her outstanding direction of the senior
play presented last night; to Dick Grumm as
coach of the football team who beat Olson High
21-20 on Friday; to Frances Cole who had done
outstanding work in measuring behavioral
objectives in teaching music; or to Larry
Hornbaker, the gardener, who had the lawn and
flower beds in beautiful condition.

Hopefully everyone can "earn" an orchid
at least once a year. It makes use of

"positive reinforcement" concepts, should
improve morale, and emphasizes the positive
instead of the negative. Possible criticism
is that it is just an expansion of the old
"gold star" reward idea used in Sunday School
class for memorizing verses in the Bible.

It is better not to award an orchid to
anyone on any given day than to give it to
someone who really doesn't deserve
one. This cheapens the concept and makes
it meaningless.

Obviously the orchid concept can be used
also in larger districts in house organs,
weekly news bulletins, and other means.

Why not give it a try--as your idea,
not ours?

THE HIDDEN AGENDA

It is best in most instances to be
direct in conversation, let people know where
you stand, get to the point, and don't beat
around the bush. On the other hand many
people don't follow this advice and the only
way you can tell what they are really saying
is to read between the lines.

A story told on a third party who talks
too much may well be a hint to you not to talk
so much. Questions at a board meeting regarding the price paid for a 50 foot length
of garden hose or the cost of lawn fertilizer
may really not be concerned with the cost.
Instead it may be a probe to see if you know
what is going on, or it may indicate a lack
of confidence in purchasing procedures. Concern expressed regarding the suspension of a

"Mexican" youth may not be about the suspension but about your attitude toward Mexican-Americans. A flowery compliment regarding a point you make regarding bilingual education may really be saying, "You have not stressed this enough in the past and thank goodness you are finally waking up to this. I'm over-complimenting you so maybe you'll get on the ball in the future."

I'm trying to see if there's a hidden agenda up there!

An agenda item requested by a board member asking information regarding dismissal procedures really may be saying, "When are you going to have enough guts to recommend dismissal of our incompetent teacher whom we all know is completely no good?"

As any good point is observed, it can be used to extreme. In looking for the hidden agenda, if you become mistrusting and suspicious regarding all comments, it would be better to forget this point entirely. Don't be like the two psychiatrists who passed each other in the hospital corridor and each said, "Good morning." After passing each said to himself, "I wonder what he really meant by that." On the other hand, if he just grunts, "Mornin'," he may be telling you something!

ARE YOU A GOOD SALESPERSON?

All educators are salesmen or saleswomen, either good, bad, or indifferent whether they recognize it or not. Teachers sell learning. Administrators sell good organization, management, inspiration to do a good job, and reasons for the general public to support the schools.

As administrators we make many mistakes in salesmanship. Sometimes we over-sell. When we have our point accepted by the school board, PTA, or teachers' group, we should quit talking. Any additional comments may unsell what we have already sold.

As administrators we are sometimes guilty of misrepresenting our product. Like large

WHO ME? A SALESMAN?

corporations which have done the same on TV
and in newspaper advertising, the penalties
may be serious. Some administrators have
told their school publics that they are providing "education in depth, superior and outstanding schools, and quality education."
Then testing scores are released showing the
average achievement for the district is at
the 40 percent level. Also, in endeavoring
to sell a tax election, we all of a sudden
tell the public things are bad and more money
is needed. The result is that the public
loses confidence in the schools and in the
administration.

Sound criteria for us to use in salesmanship include: Honesty, continuous selling
rather than just at tax election time, brief
statements--don't talk too much, admit weaknesses, use visual approaches, use facts
rather than emotions, and keep the presentations simple rather than giving complicated
and detailed information.

- - -

*Whenever possible, don't surprise the
board or staff with an important decision
which must be made immediately. Gradually
building up your case and laying proper ground-
work for anticipated needs is better than
coming up with a bag full of surprises.*

Let's agree to disagree--and be friends, anyway!

LOVE YOUR CRITICS

It would be nice if you could be an able
administrator and have everyone love you.
This is not possible and if you administer
by running a popularity contest, you are doomed
to failure. If you do anything worthwhile,
you will irritate some and if you do nothing,
you'll irritate others. Many times you must
stand up and be counted and in so doing you
will incite animosity of others.

What can be done with a colleague or a
town person who you learn is saying false,
mean, and cutting things about you? It is a
temptation to retaliate and get "even" or to
sue for defamation of character. This nearly
always will be a mistake. Another thought is
to ignore it and say, "I won't stoop to answer,"
or "I'll just turn the other cheek."

Handling such cases is situational and
no hard-bound rule can or should be given to
follow always. However, the following plan
will work in many instances and it is recommended for your consideration.

You approach the "enemy" rather than
having him come to you. You say, "Leo, you
have a wonderful wife in Bobbie and two fine
children and you have done great work with the
Little League." (Hopefully you can find a few
such positive things you can say truthfully.)
"Leo, you and I disagree on the school bus
routes (or high school athletics, or the
school tax rate, or whatever the issue is).

I wonder if we cannot agree to disagree on this issue and expect to oppose each other on it. However, I hope we both (say "both" even though you are innocent) can avoid personal remarks and criticism. Thus maybe we may never really love each other, but we can live and be in the same community without hatred for each other and probably everybody will respect both of us more. Furthermore, if I've said or done anything to offend you personally, I'm sorry. I still would like to count you as a friend even though we'll probably never agree on _____. How about it? Will you shake hands on this?"

This may not work, and in some situations should not be tried. In many cases it will work, and should be considered as one means for solving the problem.

WE HAVE A PROBLEM

One good way to correct an employee is to say, "We have a problem. Your performance is great, your reports are on time and accurate. Now our one problem we need to work on is _____."

We prefer this type of approach to: "What in the hell is_____?"

- - -

Have you complimented someone today in your organization who deserves it?

HEAR BOTH SIDES

The following is a true story that
actually happened in a small community. It
is described, altering the situation
slightly to avoid embarrassment to living
persons.

Coach John Innocent took Chris, his
pregnant wife, to the Ice Follies the evening
prior to his birthday. Both he and his wife
hoped the baby would be born on his birthday.
The doctor and his wife accompanied them to
the Ice Follies which would conclude at mid-
night. It was planned that all would go to
the hospital after the show and labor would
be induced since the baby was definitely over-
due. At the intermission the doctor suggested
that he and Chris remain seated while the other
two go for cokes for all of them. This they
did and returned within five minutes. However,
while standing in line to purchase the drinks,
the doctor's wife patted John on the shoulder
and put her arm around him urging him "to
quit worrying--all will be O.K.--my husband
has never lost a husband yet." Mrs. Gossiper,
wife of a school board member, observing the
scene from a distance was infuriated, not
knowing who the good looking woman was with
Coach Innocent.

The show ended. The trip to the hospital
was made and John Innocent, Jr. was born at
3:00 a.m. However, Mrs. Gossiper spread the
word through the school and the community the
next day that "Coach Innocent was out on a
wild date the night his wife gave birth to a
son in the hospital on his birthday." Before

73

the day was over Coach Innocent observed
friendly congratulations he had been receiving
were changed to aloofness, cold stares, the
silent treatment, and downright rudeness.

John went to the principal and asked,
"What is going on around here?" When he was
told of the concern of everyone for his behavior
on the previous night, John was beside himself.
Not until he explained the situation in a
letter to the Editor which was published two
days later in the local weekly newspaper did
the faculty and the community have renewed
confidence in their capable coach.

The moral might well be: The school
administrator believes only half of what he
sees and only one-fourth of what he hears.
He avoids judgment until he has heard both
sides of a situation. Usually there are two
sides to everything.

Believing nothing you hear and half of
what you see applies frequently. TV detec-
tives prove our point repeatedly. Every
employee has a right to tell his side of the
story before you make a judgment.

Don't jump to conclusions. See and
hear both sides first. Be like the conservative rancher riding in a car with another who
said, "I see Kenneth Lee has sheared his
sheep." The conservative rancher replied,
"Well, he has on this side for sure."

- - -

*There are nearly always two sides to
every question or problem. Be sure to hear
both sides before making a decision even
though, after hearing one side, you feel you
know the answer.*   74

I AM PRESIDENT OF THE ROTARY CLUB

A good school administrator will be active in civic affairs and will endeavor to improve the community where he lives and works. He will be active as the situation warrants in a service club, a church, the Chamber of Commerce, and other civic organizations.

Usually in service clubs and civic organizations there are elections for the presidency and the losers are not always good losers. More than once a superintendent of schools has run into trouble by beating out a poor loser for the presidency or by having to make controversial decisions after he becomes president.

In a community lacking leadership, to refuse to be president would be a serious mistake. However, in most situations leadership (or would-be leadership) is not lacking, and you can take the position that first-line leadership may hurt both you and the school district more than it will help. The better part of valor would be to show concern and interest by freely serving on the board of directors or by accepting a committee chairmanship, but not to seek the presidency. Some administrators do so much community work the job of administering the best possible educational program is neglected or almost forgotten.

Of course, "to be or not to be" president is situational and your decision should be based on a careful analysis of the situation rather than routinely endeavoring to become a civic leader. You are already a community leader as a school administrator.

75

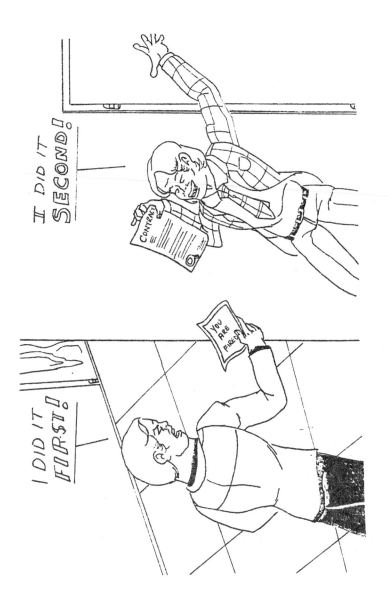

There is considerable merit in the old
saying: "Be not the first by whom the new
is tried or the last to lay the old aside."

If this were adhered to by everyone, it
would be a stark tragedy. No progress or change
would ever be made. The other extreme has
resulted by administrators who constantly
innovate just to get the reputation of being
an innovator.

An analysis of innovations since 1950
given in a recent Phi Delta Kappan Magazine
shows that most of the innovations have failed.
We would add that as many of these innovations
were discontinued, so were the services of
the administrators. Few innovations in curriculum should be made until the teachers really
want them--not just giving assent because they
are afraid to do otherwise. If you want to
spend taxpayers' money wisely and give your
pupils the best, you will let someone else
find the pitfalls in flexible scheduling,
team teaching, open classrooms, year-round
schools, teaching machines, closed circuit
television, fundamental schools, alternative
schools, and instruction by computers.

Each of the above has many fine points.
Each also has some pitfalls to be avoided.
The better part of valor is to try a pilot
study of an innovation in a few classrooms or
in one school only rather than to commit the
entire district to an unproven innovation.
Thus, you avoid loss of confidence by the
community and faculty when the innovation fails
and you don't have to leave as a self-made
martyr.

77

C. C. Trillingham, formerly an outstanding school administrator in California, has
been observed in many group meetings. A
technique he used effectively is described in
a hypothetical situation as follows:

The chairman calls the meeting to order
and announces: "We are met today to see if
we can establish consensus on a cooperative
plan for special education classes in our
county. Now speak up; let's get some good
ideas out on the table."

Seemingly those who know the least speak
first and longest. One out of every three
persons typically makes a good point. After
nearly all have spoken, Dr. Trillingham would
have the advantage of having heard the strong
points as well as the weak points. He
would then say, "Mr. Chairman, we are all
impressed by Dick's fine point regarding each
district establishing just one type of specialized program. Kim's point regarding interdistrict transfers to be arranged so all types
of special education students can be handled
with no one district having to establish ten
different costly programs is excellent.
Scott's point regarding transportation in the
manner he described makes sense. Ben's idea
that our next move should be for each district
to state its preference regarding the program
it desires to offer so we can see what duplica-
tion we must avoid should be followed. Sarah
raised a good question regarding who gets the
state aid for interdistrict transfers. We
cannot develop a standard contract for all to
use until we know the answer to the state aid.

I wonder if we can agree that we do favor the idea of a cooperative plan. I suggest the chairman appoint a committee to tell us at the next meeting about transportation ideas, another to tell us how the state aid will work, and still another committee to work on a standard contract form. I will pause here and if there is no further question, I will make the motion that we proceed accordingly.

Dr. Trillingham always pulled things together, thought and planned clearly, and exerted real leadership. But he was not the first to speak.

Of course if everyone waited for someone else to speak first, then silence would reign supreme--but human nature being such as it is, there is no danger of that!

GET THE BAD GUY INSIDE

Unless your community is different you have a few bad guys--anti-school, anti-taxes, and anti-you. We believe it is better to have one bad guy on a committee, in the PTA, or on the school board than to have him fighting on the outside. If he is inside, it gives the good guys a chance to educate him. They will work harder when they see and hear the opposition, and then everyone will know what he is up to.

Of course there are many exceptions to this idea. Maybe you need to consider this as one possible plan in your situation.

We meet next time on the tenth at four at the Eighth
Street School. No, let's change that to the fourth
at ten at the Twelfth Street School. On third
thought - - -

CHANGING DATES AND DECISIONS

A two or three day retreat for principals and district administrators is an excellent
practice and is strongly recommended. One district planned such a retreat for administrators
on Friday, Saturday, and Sunday a week before
school was to open. However, the superintendent
learned two weeks before the announced date
that half the administrators would not attend
due to the high cost of accommodations, vacations, sickness, etc. The superintendent wrote
to each administrator giving two-weeks notice
cancelling the retreat. Seven people went to
the appointed place (mountain resort 100 miles
from the district) for the retreat anyway.
They were on vacation trips and did not check
the mail at home but went directly to the
retreat only to find the affair was cancelled.
They were upset because they had cut their
vacations short, had entailed extra expense,
and had found themselves off in the mountains
without reservations.

The point is: Don't set the date, time,
and place for a meeting until you know it can
and will be held. Then having done so, stick
with it if at all possible. When you change
dates and places of meetings, it causes confusion. People wonder if you know what you are
doing. It causes inconveniences when people
have built other plans around the first announced
date and it is changed.

The same applies to decisions in general.
Examples are: opening and closing dates of
school, Christmas vacation period, dates
report cards will be issued, when certain

reports will be due, what to do in case of a fire drill, a teachers' meeting, and arranging for a substitute when ill.

We would like to say, "Having made a decision, stick with it by all means." This, however, is not realistic for unusual conditions will arise that cannot be foreseen. Changes have to be made and only a fool will stick with a decision and not admit he made a mistake; that circumstances beyond his control necessitated a change.

INTERRUPTIONS

A special note sent to a teacher during a class causes at least a loss of 30 minutes of instructional time (30 pupils for 1 minute). A doctoral dissertation shows such interruptions are unbelievably high and consequences are very bad.

An interruption during a conference may upset a whole decision almost reached. In the office, telephone interruptions are just as disruptive as people coming in and out of the office during a conference.

Once each year a campaign is needed to stop unnecessary interruptions in classes and offices.

- - -

A good administrator and conversationalist is one who listens more than he talks.

CLASSIFIED VERSUS CERTIFICATED

In most situations classified personnel cost less than certificated personnel. Many times classified employees will handle details, routines, and exacting performance better than certificated people could.

Analyze your situation. If there are eight certificated district office employees and six classified employees, maybe you need to reshuffle and have six certificated and eight classified. Just because this is the way it is now does not mean it should be continued. Each time you are tempted to add a certificated middle-management administrator, make sure you have determined first the true need for certification.

YOUR SECRETARY

As an administrator you probably associate with your secretary more than any other person in your professional life. Treat her courteously and with respect. Don't forget "thanks," "please," "that's great work." She is not just "hired help" to be ordered around. She can make or break you and can help make your life pleasant or almost unbearable. Treat her as a lady, working with you rather than for you.

CHOOSE YOUR PROBLEM

   We all have problems and you wouldn't be
happy if you did not. Surely a few problems
will be tossed at you in heaven just to make
it heaven. Maybe hell is a place with no
problems, no concerns, no interests, and
nothing to do except to idle time away.

Take your pick! Which one will you fight? One man
is 250 lbs. at 6'2" and the other is 140 lbs. at 4'6"

But back to present reality. One administrator sounded off in his community on "Federal aid for private schools." It was not even a concern or issue in his community until he made it a big one.

Another fought a straw man regarding "religion in the schools" only to find he had divided the district on an issue that had not existed before.

Any superintendent who will not stand up and be counted on a real issue affecting the schools is respected by no one. He does not, however, need to go about creating problems so he can take a stand and be counted.

One wise superintendent when asked by the press soon after his new appointment what his stand was going to be on UNESCO, sex education, and use of union workers on school construction contracts answered, "These are policy decisions which the board, not I, will make. I will bring the board the facts, consult with them and work with them. Once a decision is made, I will execute it to the best of my ability. In the meanwhile I will not prejudice the case by sounding off on my own." The press approved his stand and lauded his position.

However, a few days later he did take an immediate and strong stand publicly regarding the assault on a black teacher by a group of whites. He chose the right problem to face and the right time--immediately.

Choose your problems--don't make them!

LOOK FOR A LOST GEM IN A CAVE

Full many a gem of purest ray serene
the dark unfathomed caves of ocean bear:
Full many a flower is born to blush unseen,
and waste its sweetness on the desert air.

I'm wasting my fragrance on the desert air!

Thomas Gray probably was not concerned about school administrators when he wrote those beautiful lines, but he left a message for us anyway.

Part of the reason you are where you are today is because some professor or kind administrator during your early years recognized your potential and went out of his way to help you. "It is not only what you know but also who you know" is a true statement in this modern competitive world.

We get so absorbed in "making good" and advancing, we unintentionally let rare gems lie in caves and let flowers waste their fragrance on the desert air. It is easy to help the son of a board member or the daughter of a church friend, while we may let go unnoticed someone with great ability but without "connections."

Many a person around us rises to prominence due to his own brashness, being "pushy," or being a little "cocky." He may or may not deserve the advancements he gets. On the other hand there is in every university graduate class in school administration and in every school district at least one person with great promise. Unless you (or someone) takes an interest and helps that person "get a break," the odds may be against his or her advancement. The good, warm feeling you will have inside by helping will be more than ample reward for your trouble.

The authors feel rather strongly on this point for each of us would not have gone as far as we have if persons in bygone years had not practiced this philosophy for us. We hope you, too, will buy it.

I don't care if I have to wait all day!

You have twelve appointments for fifteen minutes each scheduled in your office during the day. This will be a total of three hours. It is probable each person will arrive five or ten minutes early. You may have to be five minutes late with several of them because you could not conclude the previous appointment. The result is that important people will tend to wait about ten minutes each in your office. It would have been better to have scheduled a ten-minute gap between each appointment so no one waited and so you have a breather.

A secretary can tell you, "Dina Brock is here," which helps to accelerate things. When the appointment is made she also can politely state, "We have available just 15 minutes from 9:45 to 10:00. Will that be acceptable?" You no doubt have your own techniques to help terminate conferences with proper tact.

But let's worry now about those important people who spend ten minutes waiting in your outer office. They are not happy about it and it might keep your secretary from working because they talk to her. Possible answers include: Have the waiting lounge chair located so the secretary will not be bothered easily after the visitor is seated; the chair should be comfortable and perhaps a cup of coffee should be offered; a magazine or recent school district report can be available.

Of course the person may be one you want to go all out for. Thus the secretary will show him or her around and entertain the person as well as possible. The least you can

do is say when coming out of your office,
"I am sorry I kept you waiting."

In summary, try not to keep people
waiting, but when you do, then have a previous
plan determined with your secretary that
covers what happens while people wait.

I LIKE TO HEAR MY NAME

We all like to hear our own names. If
you are to attend a meeting and you are not
sure you will recall the names of people you
should know, let someone tell you in advance:
"The very pretty lady is Mrs. Grumm, the man
with the beard is Mr. Tegner, the man wearing
glasses is Mr. Horne, the baldheaded man is
Dr. Clowes, and the very tall blonde is Mr.
Murdy." During the meeting, in responding to
questions, answer them by using the name of
the person who asks the question.

The practice of using people's names
and looking them in the eyes while talking
is always sound.

- - -

*We hope you are opposed to sex or race
discrimination. If you are, it is better
to show it by actions rather than by talking
about it constantly. After too much talk,
people will wonder if you are really sincere
or just a talker covering up true feelings.*

90

In conducting a public meeting on a controversial issue you may expect to be faced by an expert heckler. One of the authors in his younger days as a county administrator conducted a formal hearing with an older colleague regarding the annexation of a poor one-room country school district to a wealthy four-teacher district. The latter was willing to accept the poor district. The young administrator was interrupted by a heckler and was told, "Why don't you city slickers quit lying and go back to your offices in Los Angeles and leave us alone?" The young man, not knowing just what to say hesitated, and the older and more experienced colleague offered to handle the situation. He rose and smilingly said, "Let us all be thankful we live in the United States of America where by our Constitution we have freedom of speech and this good man can say just what he thinks about us with no fear of reprisal or recrimination. We appreciate your comments, though we may not agree with you completely."

In such a situation the sentiment of the crowd is generally with the local individual rather than with outside strangers on the stage. The polite and courteous handling of the situation caused an immediate switch of good feeling to the visiting officials. The final result was a successful annexation urgently needed.

Ordinarily you do not keep a crowd with you if you fight an individual in the audience by putting him in his place or by insulting

him. A soft answer does turn away wrath.
Think through in advance how you would
handle the heckler, the insulting dissenter,
or the town drunk who insults you in an open
meeting. Your technique can make or break
the situation.

In answering a question some administrators start by saying, "That is certainly
a good question." Avoid this by all means.
It appears to be condescending and talking
down to the very person you want to impress.
It gives the idea that other questions were
not good--that you are almost surprised a
good question was asked.

Answers should be brief and to the
point. Don't make a speech on each point.
Use a paragraph answer instead of a whole
chapter (or even a sentence instead of a
paragraph). In your enthusiasm to get to
the point, never, no never, interrupt a
person. This is like saying, "Quit talking,
I want to demonstrate my wisdom."

- - -

*When you do a favor for someone, don't
rush to tell them so "you can get credit for
it." Thus probably only one out of five
will ever know you did it but it will have
ten times the effect, so mathematically you
come out ahead anyway--and have a nice warm
feeling regarding all five cases.*

The following represent situations which you have experienced, but hopefully are not ones you have caused.

You probably have been called by a person you are not really enthused about talking with in the first place and then in the second place you are told by his secretary, "Please hold the phone while I locate Mr. Rude."

Ken Lee makes an appointment with you at 10:30 a.m. and he shows up promptly but you are on the telephone and he is told, "Please wait." And then after he is ushered into your office, the conference is interrupted three times while you take incoming telephone calls.

Have you been asked to return a toll charge phone call when you return to the office and your district is left to pay the charge?

Have you returned a call to Mr. Busy and been told to hold please, he is on the other line? Then you were told at the end of two minutes: "Mr. Busy will talk to you now."

On the other hand when placing a call to another person do you or your secretary say, "Mrs. Gladys Fergus is calling Helen Jones regarding the purchase of a lawnmower?"

Does your secretary in screening your calls do so in a manner so as not to irritate the caller?

93

Do you leave your office after you have had the secretary place a call without cancelling it? When you leave the office, do you tell your secretary where you are going? Do you have your secretary make local calls you could dial faster than you can "buzz" her and have her do it? Have you ever had a telephone company representative give a brief lesson to your staff on the use of the telephone?

We trust proper use of telephones in your district enhances the public relations image for your district.

Hold the phone, please!

94

PART III

ADMINISTRATIVE PROCEDURES

95

I'm getting with that decentralization business!

DECENTRALIZE IS THE NAME OF THE GAME

You probably remember as a beginning
administrator how you spent the first year
pulling everything into your office; in-
sisting on initialing or signing many documents; employees could not act without your
approval; and you became a first-class
bottleneck. The second year you probably
spent much time trying to get rid of "all
this mess" and wondered why "you had to do
all the work around here."

A good rule of thumb is to delegate
decision making to the lowest level possible
capable of making the decision. Thus civic
center use of a school building should not
be handled in the business manager's office
but by the appropriate principal and in
routine cases by her or his secretary on
the basis of board policies. A broken
window at the Shepherd School should be
handled by a phone call from the school to
the Head of Maintenance rather than a work
order sent to the superintendent or business
manager. Likewise, most transportation
problems should be handled by the Head of
Transportation.

A $25,000 a year principal should be
able, if you let him, to decide the answers
to four out of five of the telephone call
questions he usually makes to your office.
As you delegate responsibility, be sure you
also give necessary authority. Remember,
however, you must support, whenever possible,
the delegated decision, and in the end you
must accept the criticism for all delega-
tions that go wrong.

As you decentralize keep an open system
of "information points" so you are auto-
matically informed of what is going on in
your district. You don't have to decide
everything but you do need to know what has
been decided in many instances. Poor
decision making and weak spots will show up
to you before the crisis stage is reached
and necessary adjustments can be made for
those who cannot accept delegation.

REGARDING INDIVIDUAL DIFFERENCES

The school administrator may get the
best work from some few employees through use
of fear. Thus they are kept off balance,
wonder about job security, and are supervised
closely.

A large number of employees do their
best work if given praise frequently and
are reassured they are doing a fine job,
that they are wanted, and that they are very
much appreciated. Love seems to be the key
word for them.

Still others have no fear regarding job
security nor do they want constant praise--
they look at praise as back-slapping and
almost as an insult to their intelligence.
Incentive is the key word. They work best
when better pay and promotions are dangled
before them.

Sincerity is the word that describes
the real professional. Use of fear, close
supervision, excessive praise, and dollar
incentives are not the way in dealing with
them. Instead they appreciate being trusted,
being left alone, having a feeling of

98

belongingness, having a part in decision
making, and being a team person. They
appreciate having authority and responsibility delegated to them and a feeling
they are to a large extent their own boss.

The problem of the administrator is
to study employees and learn their "work
philosophy." If it is poor, some effort
should be made to help them develop sound
job attitudes. However, this may be
impossible. Your job, until change is
made, is to deal with them on the level
they are now on and endeavor to raise them
to a higher level. Do not deal with all
employees in the same way--recognize the
individual differences and do some adjusting yourself while you are endeavoring to
adjust them.

ON VISITING SCHOOLS

A highly successful superintendent,
when he accepted his present position, told
the board before signing the contract he
would report to his office at 9:30 each
morning. He quickly relieved the concern
of the board members by saying, "I will
report to one of the schools at 8:00 o'clock
and my secretary will know where I am. It
will not be 'visitation,' but a chance for
me to see and settle some problems with the
school principal on his home ground. I
also will be able to talk with teachers,
custodians, and cafeteria workers and get
the feel of what is going on in a far better
manner than I can by just sitting in my
office."

The plan worked beyond his greatest
expectations. He learned to know people,
particularly the classified, by their first
names. In some schools he had coffee with
the custodians before others arrived (with
the principal's knowledge and assent).
Within a year he knew more school employees
than any previous superintendent, and more
employees knew him as "one of the good guys"
rather than just as another school superintendent. The idea of going to the principals brought them closer to him. He was
able to solve many problems on the spot
without use of memos and red tape.

The press published his plan of late
arrival at his office in a very complimentary manner so the whole community knew not
to contact his office until 9:30. Speaking
to another superintendent who was using the
late arrival plan, he in effect said the
following: "Tell others to try it. It
really works, but warn them not to wait
until they get caught up at the office or
they will never start. Having once started,
don't make exceptions but do it everyday
regardless of how busy you think you are."

SAME SPEECH TWICE

More than one good public speaker
throws his notes away after each speech so
he will not give that same speech again.
He will keep in his office factual data and
jokes in a file marked "Speeches" but it
contains no speech outlines.

One teacher said to another, "Are you
going to hear Dr. Repetition speak tonight?"
The other answered, "No, I've heard his talk."

You will not give the same speech a
second time as well as you did the first
time.   Our four "S's" of good speech are:

Stand up

Speak up

Shut up

Shred it!

And that concludes this speech for today . . . .

Is this the right time to pass?

NOW IS THE TIME--OR IS IT?

A high school boy is smart enough to
know while his father is busy paying
Christmas bills or making out his income
tax not at that time to ask for an increase
in his allowance. The baseball player who
went hitless and made three errors today
can find a better time later to give the
manager some pointers.

Time is situational and thus no exact
formula can be presented for its proper use.
There is a wrong and right time to call a
bond or tax issue election. Probably the
best time is early October soon after the
opening of school and before the accumula-
tion of problems for the year has taken
effect. Probably the worst time is within
a month of payment of property taxes, income
taxes, Christmas, spring vacation, at the
same time as a state or national election
or a local school board election. Just
before the end of the school year or during
summer vacation are also poor election dates.

We don't ask teachers to put in a
longer day just after their salary request
is refused, nor do we ask the school board
to increase administrative salaries at
that time.

Proper timing is something that you
have to learn to feel, and it is partly
intuitive. It is probably one of the most
neglected concepts by practicing administrators.

If timing is taken so seriously that
there is never a "right time" to do things
which must be done, then perpetual pro-
crastination results and "do nothing"
administration results.

Usually there is a right time--or at
least a better time. Your job is to weigh
all factors and determine the best time.
If you are not convinced, read the topic
entitled "Sense of Timing" in Part I again.

WE NEED A POLICY ON THAT

One of the best legacies a successful
administrator can leave behind him is sound
policies developed on a cooperative basis.
If he (she) answers the same question several
times in a month, a policy is needed to make
decision making automatic. All who are
affected by a policy should participate
(not determine) in the development of the
policy. A sound policy developed solely
by the administration and issued as an edict
will have tough sailing, if accepted at all,
while a less desirable policy developed on a
"we" basis will prove better.

Consideration of extending sick leave
from seven days to ten days a year for
classified employees should be referred to
the classified organization for study first.
A requirement that all teachers shall remain
in their classrooms for at least fifteen
minutes after the close of school likewise
should be referred to the teachers' organiza-
tion(s) first.

Now, let's see. . . . Do we have a
    policy on this?

The day of the benevolent despot is gone.
Administration by policies cooperatively
developed is here to stay. Dr. S. C. Joyner,
formerly Deputy Superintendent of Los Angeles
City Schools and a great administrator, once
remarked, "I want policy development to reach
the point so when the phone rings and I'm
asked a question all I have to do most of the
time is to think what policy covers that
point or I can say to myself we need to start
policy development to cover that point in the
future." Greater efficiency, better use of
time, and provision of more equitable justice
all result from administration by policies.

Don't wait until you have a whole book of
policies to adopt--do it on the piecemeal
approach and realize it is a continuous project. One policy adopted means a good start
has been made.

And the most important policy of all is
to provide an established procedure permitting
needed exceptions to policies in order to take
care of the unusual or crisis situation.

THE RIGHT WAY TO WRITE A REPORT

All administrators write reports. News-
papers try to tell in the first paragraph
"who, what, when, and where." Organismic
psychology stresses getting the picture of
the "whole" first and then analyzing the parts
later.

Observing these sound principles, you
should in the first sentence of a board report
say for example, "It is recommended that a
new 16mm motion picture projector be purchased

Please give me a sheet of paper. I want to write a
board report.

immediately at a cost of $1500 from the Duke Audio-Visual Company. This amount was budgeted; the old projector is beyond repair and the proposed replacement represents the lowest quotation received for a projector of similar specifications." Then if the administrator feels the urge to do so, he can expand on the use which will be made of the projector, the hours per day it will be used and by how many different teachers, and whatever else is appropriate.

Too often a report uses inductive reasoning and builds up a long case and the reader skips to the last paragraph to see what the conclusion will be. Why not give the conclusion first? Give the overall picture first and maybe the reader needs no more facts than the initial summary. Few reports should exceed one page in length. Detailed facts should be available in supplementary sheets, if requested, but in most instances they will not be desired. Instead of seeing how long a report you can write, strive to see how short you can make it.

Another type of report could begin: "It is recommended that the eight teachers listed below be granted tenure effective July 1 and the other two shown be given notice in accordance with board policy and state law that their services will not be required after June 30." All the details regarding previous evaluations, classroom visitations, and administrator-teacher conferences may be supplied separately, if requested. Of course observance of state laws always takes precedence.

In summary, get to the point first, give the overall picture and keep it all to one page, when possible, typewritten and double spaced, but have detailed supplementary data available if requested.

We hope your district already has a policy which includes the following ingredients:

1. When a person announces his candidacy for the school board, the superintendent shall contact him immediately. He shall invite him to his office and give him such things as annual reports, board policies, copy of the budget, financial reports, and factual data. He will tell the candidate that for the good of the district and in accordance with board policy, the superintendent will stay out of taking sides in the election.

2. The candidate will be given a pamphlet approved by the board but probably prepared by some outside leader, preferably a board member. It should cover recommended "do's" and "don'ts" for all candidates and urge them not to tear down the district as a means of getting elected--to keep their campaign on issues rather than on personalities, and not to become obligated particularly to school employees or associations, and not to make campaign promises they may later not want to keep.

You will be tempted, if he is anti-schools to greet him/her cooly--don't do it! He may be one of your new bosses. Treat him in a friendly manner and as you would want to be if you were in his position.

You will be tempted to do too much if he is an "extra" good candidate. Don't do it! If he is elected he will respect you more if he knows you are a square shooter and not one who engages in board elections.

Once in a lifetime the situation may
arise when you believe it is proper and a must
for you to take a strong stand in a board
election. Before you do, think through the
consequences if you lose. If you are going
to be involved, do it with professional
dignity.

"I'm going to run for the school board.
Are you going to support me?"

"Well, errr.... uhhh... let me think."

This book is intended for administrators and graduate students who are planning to become administrators. Possibly points made here can be made by someone to new board members.

As a new board member you should remember that primarily you are one only in board meetings and you do not issue orders or requests to employees as all such should be made by administrative action. Any board request should be by official board action and not by separate individuals. You are now a representative of the state serving your local community and most of what you can or cannot do is governed by state law or regulation. Education is a state function.

Get all the facts and know both sides before you start trying to make a lot of changes. Schools are big business, and probably the largest business in your city. On the other hand, school districts are different from ordinary business and they are not operated for profit. Thus all good business procedures are not applicable to school districts.

If you decide to run for the school board just to cut the tax rate; to get the science teacher fired; get a new coach; throw some business to a relative; get away from a dominating wife or husband; to improve your declining business; or as a first step toward a political career, then you have made a mistake. Real quick like, determine to serve your community by way of providing good schools, or resign.

You may have a weak superintendent but
the chances are he is a very able man. Back
him when you can and when you disagree with
his recommendations go all out to be sure
you are doing the right thing. Don't let the
little group who worked to elect you do your
thinking for you.

Be sure you have no conflict of interest
in any actions the board takes. Remember
you represent all the people (race, creed,
color, politics, religions, rich, and poor).
Move very slowly the first six months and do
a lot of listening. Don't be ashamed to say,
"I'm sorry I don't understand this and before
I vote I would like to have it explained
again." Remember you are a community representative, an appraiser, and a policymaker.
You are not an administrator--that is the job
of your superintendent. If you want to be an
administrator, you selected the wrong job.

Please don't get your feelings hurt
because we spoke plainly. The above is for
about 10 percent only and the strong odds
are you are to be thanked sincerely for what
you are doing in rendering this great service.

HOW ABOUT THAT NEW SCHOOL BOARD MEMBER?

Again, we hope your district has policies
that include:

1. The board president will write a
letter of congratulations to the newly
elected board member and urge him/her to
attend all meetings (as a spectator only)
until he or she takes office.

2. The board president will offer to include in the agenda of one of those board meetings an executive session to discuss and explain anything desired by the newly elected board member, provided state law permits this in executive session.

3. The superintendent will invite the newly elected board member to meet with him and his cabinet to ask questions and/or receive further indoctrination regarding the district.

It is to be hoped that the state school board association (or an intermediate unit) has meetings in various locations for newly elected board members.

One of the five most important jobs a school superintendent has is to help "educate" new board members. This job should be taken seriously. He may keep the new board member from making a fool of himself and from hurting the district if he helps to orient the new board member with care and caution. The authors have observed many superintendents who handled new board members (who had announced before elected they would get the superintendent fired) in such a way they became one of his strongest supporters.

Don't ignore the newly elected board member even though you think he is your enemy or the district's antagonist.

- - -

You will probably be judged as an administrator three-fourths on what you are and one-fourth on what you do. Conduct is the largest concern of the school administrator.

113

SOCIALIZING WITH THE SCHOOL BOARD

Should you or should you not as a
superintendent socialize with the school
board members? Custom and expectancies of
the past in your district may give you the one
and only answer and you don't need to read
any further.

A good practice is once or twice a year
to entertain the entire board and their
spouses, as well as your assistant superintendents and their spouses. Then in general
stop right there! A return engagement to the
homes of each of the board members is to be
anticipated.

Forming a social group including only a
part of the board is to be avoided with certainty.
Usually it is best to get your social plan out
on the table so no one misunderstands what you
are doing. If you are already a close personal
friend of a newly elected board member, your
friendship need not cease, but good tact in
avoiding appearance of favoritism is appropriate.

The size of your district will determine
whether or not you should have another social
affair for principals and/or central office
personnel. Experience indicates the best
way to hold your job is being a competent
administrator rather than by depending on
social functions.

As a school principal or other administrator, you should avoid entertaining the board
members. Your social activities might well be
patterned after the above plan but at the
school level and for all your school personnel (both certificated and classified).

114

In summary, there is no simple answer to
this question and the solution will vary
between schools and districts. Think through
your own situation and act accordingly. It
is better to "under do" than to "over do."

Did they say we were not to socialize? Surely
they didn't mean this--I hope!

REGARDING THE BOARD AGENDA

An entire chapter of a textbook is needed to cover this topic adequately. Maybe the following points might stimulate thinking and be of help.

1. The board agenda should be received by board members either two or three days in advance of a board meeting.

2. It should include for each item all pertinent data, arguments for, possible arguments against, financial impact if any, and a proposed motion.

3. The minutes of the last meeting should be reproduced so it is unnecessary to read them aloud at the meeting. Approval of the minutes should be the first agenda item.

4. The second agenda item should be "Financial" and should include submission of financial reports. The "Financial" item should include a report of purchase orders and contracts by number so all can be approved or ratified by one motion.

5. The third section of the agenda should be "Personnel." It should include separately numbered personnel reports so all resignations can be accepted as one motion, proposed employments as another, approval of overtime as another, etc.

6. Other sections should deal with curriculum and instruction, transportation, new construction, maintenance and operations, food services, etc.

7. Some agenda items should be information items which in most cases are read before the meeting and no action is needed.

8. When a good agenda procedure is used and board meetings are handled as described later in "Three Aspects of School Board Meetings," then it becomes possible to include an additional agenda item: a 30-minute presentation for information purposes of some phase of the educational or business phase of the district's program.

9. Finally, don't get carried away. Don't make the agenda any longer than necessary. Most agendas we see are either grossly inadequate, or more often entirely too long.

REGULAR, SPECIAL, AND ADJOURNED

BOARD MEETINGS

There are only three general kinds of school board meetings.

A regular board meeting is one regularly scheduled on some such date as the first and third Mondays at 7:30 p.m. in the district offices.

A special board meeting is one called in accordance with state law (by the president on 24 hours with notice to all concerned) to consider an emergency matter(s) between regular meetings. Some meetings regarding elections, bond issues, and budget approval come under this category also. Usually action may be taken only on those topics included in the call.

An adjourned board meeting is a continuance of either a regular or special meeting.

117

I cannot help you with the dishes tonight.
I must read all the facts in this Board Agenda.

The press and general public frequently resent special meetings if they are used to avoid publicity of actions or to keep things under cover. Thus they should be avoided and used as an exception only. If many special meetings are called, it indicates either poor planning or the need for an additional regular board meeting each month.

An executive session is not another type of board meeting but is an adjournment by the board from a regular, special, or adjourned meeting for a discussion of problems relating to students or employees or whatever state law permits. Such sessions may be used to protect individuals from adverse publicity or used to consider a very delicate matter. No action may be taken in an executive session since all action must be handled in a public meeting (true unless stated otherwise by state law).

All board meetings should be open to the public, and the public should be made to feel welcome even though you wish they would stay at home!

The seating arrangement for the board should not be just one long table so board members face the audience but cannot easily see each other. A wedge shaped table (or similar device) should be used so board members can confer with each other as well as be seen by the audience.

The superintendent (if he has prepared a proper agenda) needs to talk very little (and most superintendents talk too much). Staff members should be called upon by the superintendent and not by a board member if they are to be requested to answer questions.

THREE ASPECTS OF SCHOOL

BOARD MEETINGS

A successful plan used in a number of districts is described, with the hope it will shorten your board meetings and use time more effectively.

After the meeting is called to order, flag salute, roll call, and approval of the minutes of the last meeting, the rest of the meeting, like all Gaul is divided into three parts.

The first is the Hearing Session. Upon arrival each person receives a one page listing of agenda items. The president states that the board is glad to listen to comments not to exceed three minutes in length from any individual, and the total for all speeches shall not exceed one hour. Comments are then invited on the first agenda item, then the second, and so on. Regardless of how vicious the comments are, the board resists arguing with anyone as this truly is a hearing session. The president may answer briefly a factual question, but inquirers requesting detailed information are encouraged to make an appointment with the proper administrator and are assured all facts will be given freely. The hearing session is only for hearing and never for argumentation or defensive action.

The second part is the Action Session. Since the superintendent has given each board member a copy of the agenda three days in advance, time is not taken needlessly in giving information to board members at the meeting.

121

For each item arguments for the proposal,
possible arguments against, all pertinent
factual information needed, and a proposed motion prepared by the superintendent
are included in the agenda. As an agenda
item comes up, a board member may ask further
questions or before voting he may make any
comments he feels are needed resulting from
comments made at the hearing session; but
in this session there is no further audience
participation. This portion of the meeting
should move swiftly and twenty ordinary items
should be handled in as little as thirty
minutes.

The meeting is then adjourned and a
recess follows, if state law permits--
otherwise adjournment will follow the third
part.

The third part is the Conference Session
and usually the audience will leave if assured
that no further action will take place. Now
the superintendent can get the thinking of
board members regarding items he must make a
recommendation on in the future; dirty linen
can be washed in private instead of public;
and all can get things off their minds they
don't care to do at a formal meeting.

Traditional, historical, and situational
factors may make it better for you to forget
this whole plan and continue as you are, but
it is believed to be worthy of your consideration.

- - -

*One caution for school administrators is not
to become too fond of the applause of the
multitude.*

122

Board minutes are the single most important legal document a district possesses and should be prepared systematically and carefully. Possibly these few selected points should be emphasized. Some of these have been recommended previously by the great leader in educational administration, Irving R. Melbo.

1. The maker and seconder of each motion should be shown and if not passed unanimously, the "yes" and "no" votes by members should be recorded. The time the meeting was called to order, the date and place of the meeting, and the time of adjournment by motion should be included. The point of arrival in relation to agenda items or departure time should be indicated for any member who is present for only a portion of the meeting.

2. The minutes should reflect all employments, resignations, dismissals, approval of all purchase orders and contracts, overtime employments, new policies, and resolutions and motions adopted or rejected.

3. The minutes should be confined to a record of actions taken and should not show comments of board members--there is no place for editorials.

One example of editorializing was a board which let a teacher go at the end of the year by formal and appropriate action. Then the board said, "This is caused by an expected decline in enrollments." This was said just to let the teacher down easy, even though they were very happy to "get rid of him." The following fall enrollments

123

I'm making a duplicate set of minutes to be
stored in a safe place in case of fire.

increased, the teacher sued for his job and was reinstated by the courts. Moral is: State the actions only--leave out the comments.

4. Have "no strings attached" such as the "building is accepted subject to approval of the architect." A board cannot give away its authority. Get the architect's approval first, and then take action. In "subject to" action, it is not known exactly when the building was really accepted and how long any mechanics' liens will have to run.

5. Likewise, if a contract is approved "subject to approval of legal counsel" or some other party, legal confusion may result. Again the board cannot give away its authority even though it desires to do so. If this were done, the completeness of the approval, the time, date, and place would be unknown. The minutes become "confounded."

6. Except in most unusual circumstances, no item should be included that is not in the agenda. State law may prohibit this anyway.

7. A duplicate set of minutes should be kept at a separate location for protection against fire, robbery, or vandalism.

- - -

We as school administrators must strive to simplify the parts of a complex organization. Read the rough draft of the report and take out the useless jargon; help cut the red tape; and remember that the schools belong to the people.

REPRESENTATIVE DEMOCRACY

In the early days of the United States, the entire community came together in the schoolhouse and decided all the questions regarding the local school.

As communities became larger, town hall meetings were replaced by selectmen and they in turn by school boards for school affairs. Thus a community said, "We cannot all meet together and decide all these things. We will elect a school board to represent us and do this for us." In this way representative democracy and control of schools evolved. The concept of the school board was enacted into law by the states. The boards receive their authority from the state. The only authority boards have is that given by the state and the state can alter or withdraw authority previously granted. Education is a state function. It is a local responsibility to provide education within the framework determined by the state.

The implications of all this for school administrators are:

1. Before making a recommendation, the superintendent should have the advantage of community thinking (the school board) before he makes recommendations instead of after. Thus the need of "Conference Sessions" as explained in the topic "Three Aspects of School Board Meetings" becomes evident in a representative democracy. In the conference sessions the superintendent gets community thinking before, instead of after, he makes his recommendations.

126

2. Employees should <u>participate</u> in
policy and decision making but should not
determine them. If employees "run" the school
district, we no longer have representative
democracy. This would mean we should go
back to the town meeting, but this of course
is not possible.

3. The <u>representative</u> board should remember it represents all the people of the com-
munity--not a segment--in performing its
state function. For this reason the authors,
except in most unusual situations, do not
favor wards or precincts for election of
board members.

INFORMATION PLEASE

"I seem to be the last one to get the
word," or "Why doesn't someone tell me these
things?" are expressions often used by administrators. A good administrator delegates
and gives necessary authority to go with
responsibility. On the other hand he still
needs to know "what is going on." Some
techniques include: information points by
routine reports, carbon copies of letters or
memos which the writer feels will interest
you, informal one or two sentence memos
addressed to you, phone calls to your secretary to tell you the following as information only "and that all is under control."

Standard information report forms can
keep you informed regarding student accidents,
pupil suspensions, employee absences, trash
can or minor fires, warehouse shortages, bus
accidents, bomb scares or integration
problems. Carbon copies of correspondence

Congratulations! You are the proud father of a nine pound baby boy.

It's about time someone told me what's going on around here!

marked "FYI" can help. One sentence memos written in long hand serve a good purpose for information items without interrupting the secretary to type them.

Whether or not you need to know warehouse shortages or bomb scare threats depends upon the level of administrative position you hold, but means are available to keep you informed regarding what you need to know without causing an undue burden on others.

Likewise, communication is a two-way process and you should consider how you can keep those working with you informed. One example of this is to have copies of approved purchase orders and work orders sent to concerned persons. Another is to have copies of board minutes (to be approved at next board meeting) posted at each school within 24 hours after each board meeting.

Misinformation and lack of information are two of the more important causes of poor employee morale and idle gossip.

TRAVEL EXPENSES

The following incidents are known to have happened and they humiliated those concerned:

1. An employee drove his car to a convention taking two other employees with him but all three claimed mileage reimbursement.

2. An employee took the district-owned car for a weekend in the mountains and had an accident.

3. An administrator taught a class one night a week at a local university and used the district car for transportation.

4. The wife of an administrator used the district car for a short trip to the grocery store and smashed the fender.

5. An administrator frequently used a district car but also received an allowance of $100 per month for transportation.

All of the above and shadows of them are to be condemned in no uncertain terms.

A school board authorized its superintendent to attend the annual state convention of school administrators with all necessary expenses to be paid by the district. The convention was held at an expensive hotel and meetings were held at breakfast, lunch, and dinner. Tickets for breakfast meetings cost $5.00; the lunch cost was $6.50, and for dinner it was $10.00. The banquet on the final evening was $12.50. The district consisted of lower middle class citizens. The editor of the local paper constantly sought to publish sensational type stories. Since expense claims and the district's bookkeeping records were public information, the editor discovered the above costs of meals and ran a story entitled, "School Superintendent Spends $24.00 in One Day of Taxpayer Money To Eat." No mention was made of the fact that the superintendent had to spend these amounts if he attended the meetings. More than one administrator has been surprised to find his expense claims published on the front page of the local paper.

I'll have a peanut butter sandwich--only.

After that experience the superintendent
turned in only those expense claims he was
willing to have published. The $50 a year
he lost was charged up in the future to income
tax deduction and to just "playing it safe."

Obviously the incident described may
never happen to you. You know the type of
community you have and whether or not the
newspaper editor is a witch hunter. Assess
your own situation and decide your course of
action as a result of thoughtful analysis
rather than by the cruel action of some
warped mind.

In any case make sure your travel expense
claims are in no way a "swindle sheet."

ARRANGING YOUR OFFICE

Superintendent Mildred Hight sat behind
the desk in her office and each person who
had an appointment with her was seated across
the desk from her in the usual seating arrangement. In thinking over the arrangement,
Mildred felt the desk between them represented
a definite barrier and her much more expensive
desk chair gave an impression of self importance and superiority. She remembered that
visitors sometimes picked up not only their
own papers brought with them, but occasionally
by mistake included others.

She conceived the idea of placing her
desk and chair in the far corner of the
office so she could turn to one side in her
swivel chair and face the visitor. Thus
there was no desk between them but instead
a small coffee table with a flower arrangement. A comfortable living room type chair

was provided for the visitor. If the
conference was to last for several minutes,
Mildred moved to another overstuffed chair.

Mildred found the results very desirable.
The cold office was changed to an informal
"den" situation. Communication was improved
and a spirit of friendliness permeated the
situation.

If you ask Mildred, now after a year's
experience, what she thinks about it she
will say, "It is great! Get rid of the desk
barrier between you and the other person.
If your office is not large enough to provide both the overstuffed chairs, the least
you can do is to see if you can place your
desk so when you turn in your chair you will
talk to the visitor with no desk barrier
between you."

DO YOU KNOW WHAT YOUR JOB REALLY IS?

Hopefully the school board has approved
a "job description" for every position used
in the school district. This is a "must" if
it has not already been accomplished. But
good job descriptions still leave a lot of
doubts. These include the business manager
who recently joined a service club, the
junior chamber of commerce, and an environ-
mental group thinking the superintendent
would be pleased only to learn the superintendent really wanted him "to quit running
around so much and be in the office more."

A school principal understood the district wanted "tough" evaluation of teachers.
He evaluated tougher than he really thought
best only to learn later this was the very
thing the superintendent wanted him to avoid.

I know where to park my car, where the cafeteria is, and the location of the executive washroom-- now I wonder what I'm supposed to DO around here . . . .!

Then there was the probationary teacher who was a strict disciplinarian, against her better judgment, because she understood this was expected by the principal if she were to receive tenure. The truth was just the opposite she learned later.

Try an experiment for yourself. Ask five people who "work for you" (hopefully "work with you") each to list three things they think you want them to do more of or work towards, and three things they are now doing they think you might like for them to do less or differently. You will be amazed at the results.

Everyone not only has a right to know what his job is, but also to know the unspoken and unwritten expectancies as well.

A prominent school superintendent and his assistant superintendent had a "falling out" because the superintendent wanted the assistant to remain quiet at school board meetings while the assistant spoke up constantly thinking he was backing up the boss and he would be pleased.

Is this a problem in your organization?

- - -

An administrator is evaluated as great based upon performance, behavior, judgments, and characteristics displayed in numerous situations and occasions. It often takes only one major foul up to shatter that image.

CONDUCTING THAT MEETING

If you are to conduct a one-hour meeting to be attended by 20 people whose average salary is $20 per hour and your own is $50 per hour, then the conference will cost at least $450. Thus it behooves you to consider the following points prior to calling the meeting:

1. Is the meeting really needed in the first place?

2. Do you have a set time to begin and to adjourn which participants know will be observed?

3. Have all persons been properly notified of the meeting and possibly reminded of it later?

4. Do you have an agenda prepared which will be supplied to each person before the meeting begins?

5. Is factual material included with the agenda so time is not wasted on time-consuming details during the meeting?

6. Are paper and pencils for note taking provided?

7. Have secretaries been requested not to interrupt the meeting with telephone calls for any one attending except in dire emergency?

8. Have the purpose of the meeting and the objectives to be reached been determined and shown on the agenda?

Now that I have called the meeting to order, does
anyone know what we want to do?

9. If you get bogged down on the first point, then admit that it cannot be settled today and move on to the next item so the meeting does not become a failure.

10. Do you endeavor to find the fine line between keeping the meeting moving, avoiding the extraneous, but at the same time not appearing to be rushed and in no case being rude to people?

11. Are minutes of the meeting needed and if so, who will record them?

12. How will communication be made to absentees?

13. Is the time and place of the next meeting announced?

Time is a very valuable commodity. If you are going to have a meeting, plan it carefully, conduct it with skill, and evaluate it in your own mind when it is concluded so future meetings will be even more successful.

AVOID ADMINISTRATION BY COMMITTEES

The concept of participatory management as expressed by Likert is a fundamental principle which every administrator should know and use. However, Share Sincerity, the assistant superintendent, did not know how to observe it. She had heard a lot about democratic administration, group decision making, shared responsibility, group dynamics, and involvement of personnel. She adopted the committee approach to decision making with the result she lost the confidence of the board, the superintendent, and the staff.

Why don't we just refer it to a committee
and then we won't have to face the issue for
another year?

Committees may be used properly to analyze, suggest, reach a compromise recommendation, and for other advisory purposes. They should not be used to make decisions. This is an abrogation of control and shirking of responsibility by some administrator.

Decisions reached by committees usually do not represent the best thinking but a compromise between the worst and the best-- which is mediocrity. Committees are time consuming, expensive in person hours, delay decision making, and weaken the administrative structure. Responsibility of the administrator cannot be avoided by blaming the result on a committee. Everyone knows you can get the decision you want by appointing the right committee members, but in so doing you are really not fooling anyone.

Share was advised she was using poor practice. She was smart enough to admit it. She changed her tactics overnight. She used an advisory council, opened two-way communication, became more approachable, invited suggestions and learned to listen twice as much as she talked. She learned to ask, "What do you think about the idea of our doing. . . ?" She also learned that many of the decisions she had been making should have been delegated to a person closer to the problem. By using these methods, better decisions came from not only Share but also from her divisions. The result was that Share Sincerity regained the confidence of all concerned and she lived happily ever after!

Now having argued against the use of committees too much, it must be admitted in some situations to infuse a "little democracy" in administration or for other good reasons, all committees should not be abolished.

ON WRITING RECOMMENDATIONS

Letters of recommendation many times cover up as much as they reveal, and there is little correlation between the superlatives in letters of recommendation and actual performance. They may not be confidential; if malice can be shown, someone may be sued. They may have been written to get rid of a poor employee; and though they will no doubt continue to be used, you will do well to supplement the written recommendations you receive by telephone calls and interviews.

Our recommended "do's" and "don'ts" include the following:

1. No one should give another as a reference unless he has received permission to do so.

2. It is better to decline the request in the first place than to agree to write a recommendation that will not help the individual.

3. An old and invalid school of thought holds that you say a few justified good things but then find at least one negative point so you will show it is not just a "whitewash." We find usually one negative point is the death sentence. If you really want to help the person, skip the negative point unless it is so serious you feel you must. However, you should never be in this position since you should have declined the request to be used as a reference in the first place.

4. You should remember "confidential" recommendations by state law, local ethics, or carelessness do not stay confidential.

141

5. If you must say a negative point, say something like this: "I regret to state Mr. X has had considerable difficulty in classroom discipline, though he has many other fine points." Now you are clearly showing "no malice."

6. Since a person today at age 25 may be entirely different at age 40, it may be appropriate to state in some cases, "This recommendation is to be destroyed after five years," or some given period of time.

Other aspects of this topic are considered in Part I under the heading of "Check the Candidates Personally."

ACCEPTING GIFTS

Board action should be required for a school district to accept any gift to the district. A very conservative board may not care to accept a picture of Franklin Delano Roosevelt for the Herbert Hoover Elementary School. Likewise, the liberal board may not want a picture of Dwight W. Eisenhower for the John F. Kennedy Junior High School. Boards and administrators can be embarrassed as a result of gifts "accepted" by a school principal, alumni group, or the student body. It may be just another white elephant. It may result in one school having equipment that others do not have with a violation of the principle of a "common" and "equal" system of education. Thus all districts should have a gift policy.

Another problem regarding gifts is those given to employees as personal gifts. A turkey given at Christmas, a weekend at

142

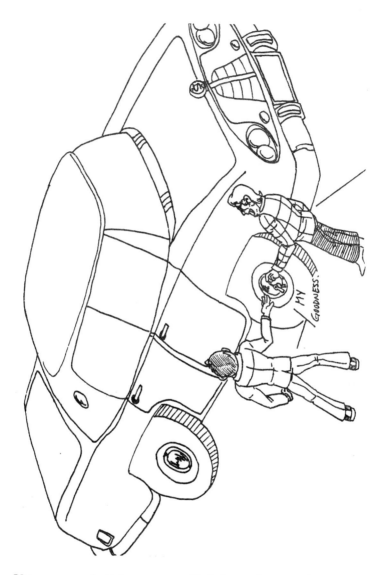

Please accept this as a small token of our esteem
and appreciation.

Catalina Island paid for by a vendor and a
Christmas check are known instances of gifts
to school administrators that received very
adverse newspaper publicity. They caused
great concern to the employees involved and
also to the school board.

An administrator of a large city school
district received an expensive electric
refrigerator at Christmas. He sent a collect
telegram to the vendor saying, "If it's a
bribe, it's too damn little. If it's a gift,
it's too damn much. Come and get it!"

It should be a board policy that no
gifts shall be accepted from vendors or
contractors by any employee. Any gift
retained shall become property of the school
district and shall be accepted by the board.

A box of candy for a secretary shared
by her with others in the office surely is
to be permitted. What to do about a gift of
a bottle of fine Scotch whiskey? It is
probably a "no-no." When in doubt, don't
accept it. It has been said that there is no
such thing as a college girl being just a
little bit pregnant. She is or she is not!

WHO STOLE THE STUDENT BODY FUNDS?

From a legal standpoint there still
exists much confusion regarding student body
funds. Minors generally cannot execute legal
contracts or make financial obligations.
Legal questions arise regarding who is
responsible in case someone is hurt at a
student body activity, who is responsible
for unpaid student body or club bills, and
who is responsible if big shortages show up

144

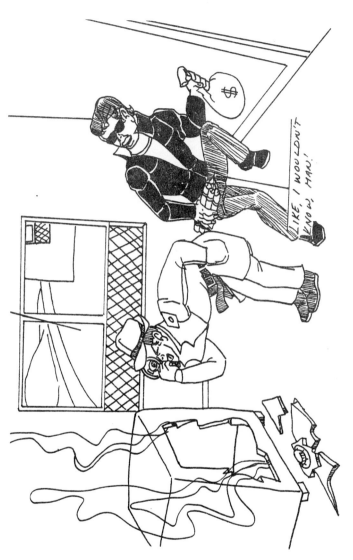

Now, who do you suppose stole the student body funds?

in student body funds. State laws and court
decisions vary between states. Keeping in
mind first your own state laws, then the
following should be considered:

1. Each club or student body organization should be approved by school board
action individually or on the basis of board
policies previously established.

2. Board policy should provide for
deposit of all funds received in a bank and
all disbursements by check signed by a
designated adult bonded school employee and
the appropriate student representative.
Student body purchase orders and contracts
should be issued in accordance with board
policy and signed by the appropriate student
representative and a designated district
employee.

3. Bookkeeping usually can be handled
more efficiently in the central district
business office than at schools. Status of
each account can be determined, if needed,
daily by telephone or by remote computer
terminal.

4. All cash should be handled by use of
cash registers equipped with a tape and total-
izer, by use of printed, prenumbered receipts
provided in duplicate with control of all
receipt books issued, or by use of printed
prenumbered tickets issued under proper control.

5. Approved fund raising activities and
types of expenditures allowed should be
included in board policy. We hope gigantic
fund raising and big-time expenditures will
not be allowed. Since the district should
provide band and athletic uniforms, these in

146

general should not be funded by the student body.

6. All food services should be provided by the district cafeteria program and student body activities should not compete with the district food service program.

7. Student body expenditures should not be allowed which will permit one school to become equipped better than another thus violating constitutional provisions of uniformity, common system of education, and equality of educational programs.

8. No paid program should be permitted on school time while state aid is being received.

9. Student body funds should be spent for social affairs, the school annual, and such--but not to replace proper district expenditures.

10. An annual audit should be required by board policy.

11. Educational values of student body leadership are great and should be encouraged to the fullest extent. Poor procedures used in handling student body funds encourage thievery, robbery, and train students in sloppy business procedures. It often ends with, "Who stole the student body funds?"

12. Parents and citizens who are constantly pressured to give money or buy tickets for student activities, or for advertisements in the school annual, get "turned off with it all" frequently. The result is poor P.R. as well as possible opposition to subsequent tax increases or bond issues.

147

CHANGING A GRADE OF "F" TO "A"

Every administrator can cite one situation where a disturbed teacher gave a straight "A" senior high school student seeking a scholarship a "C" or "F" and it obviously was a mistake or at best terrible judgment. Ethics in general prohibit an administrator from changing a grade given by a teacher. Some states have enacted laws to cover such situations. These sometimes give added protection to the teacher or in other cases better protection for a wronged pupil. An actual case where a teacher gave an "F" to every member of his class after he was notified he would not be re-employed for the following year certainly needed some previously adopted procedure for change of grades.

Thus ethics, laws, justice, academic freedom, teacher, and pupil morale all become closely intertwined. What should be done when a gross injustice has been made and state law does not cover the situation? Probably an answer similar to this can be found:

A committee can be appointed or an ombudsman selected to bring to the superintendent a recommendation (not decision) for presentation to the board--a "change of grade policy." Depending upon the local customs and background, the committee might well include the president of the high school student body, the PTA president or representative, the president of the Teachers' Association(s) or representative(s), and a high school administrator.

The policy adopted subsequently by the school board should make it possible after a review (fact finding) by a designated committee

and after a formal hearing to permit the
school principal to change a grade.

Maybe the above is not the final answer.
But the important point is that every district
should develop a policy prior to a crisis
instead of closing the gate after the cow
is in the cornpatch.

YOU SUCCEED THROUGH OTHERS

An elementary school principal was dismissed because he was "too nice a guy." He
wanted his staff to like him and he did not
want them to think he felt he was too good
to do the unpleasant jobs around school.
He spent one hour a day supervising the
cafeteria because he hated to assign this
unpleasant task to anyone else. This
included wiping up bottles of spilt milk and
keeping the youngsters reasonably quiet as
they arrived, ate, and departed.

In the presence of one of the authors he
was told by the superintendent that the district could not afford to pay $25,000 a year
for him to mop up spilt milk--that the noon
hour was an ideal time to eat and visit with
teachers and solve many minor problems outside
the office.

The principal also checked toilets
several times a day, picked up papers dropped
in the halls, adjusted sprinkler heads when
out of order, filled supply requisitions for
teachers from the school storeroom, conducted
all school assembly programs, conducted an
after-school detention room for students, and
he was really a "do it yourself" good guy.
He certainly was sincere and he was not lazy.

Who says I don't give them a day's work around here?

The next year while visiting the school it was noted there was a new principal. In response to an inquiry the superintendent said, "We had to let him go--he just couldn't learn not to mop up spilt milk. The new principal on occasions does any of the menial tasks, but as a routine all these functions are assigned to a custodian or other classified employee. Our new principal, Catherine Clark, concerns herself with improved instruction, classroom visitations, parent conferences, teacher evaluations, meeting objectives, participatory management and planning. She is respected and liked by all far more than her predecessor was--yet he was a 'nice guy!'"

Others probably won't do any job as well as you will, but you are paid to help plan, direct, and get work done through others rather than doing it yourself. This is the right way to be a nice guy and it does not mean you are lazy, insensitive, or too good to roll up your sleeves and do the dirty job on occasion. You succeed through others and with others.

DO YOU HAVE THE GUTS TO DISMISS?

Considerable research is reported in a doctoral dissertation on "Concerns of School Board Members" and it has been found that one of the chief concerns of board members is the unwillingness of superintendents to try to dismiss incompetent employees. They say too often these employees are "kicked upstairs," ignored, or maybe just transferred.

In defense of the superintendents it must be said:

1. State laws make the dismissal process almost impossible in many instances.

2. The violent opposition of employee organizations (often to clearly justified dismissals) is to be feared.

3. Legal action for damages against the accuser if the dismissal does not hold may be expected.

4. The administration may find itself more on trial than the accused.

The authors do not wish to be misunderstood. We favor sound tenure laws, contractual rights, and fair personnel policies that protect employees from injustices, discrimination, reprisals, or politics. We believe 95 percent of the teachers are doing a good job and should not be dismissed.

There are many cases, however, where superintendents "let the sleeping dog lie" when it is not necessary and when students are the real victims. The Ethics Committee, Personnel Standards Committee, or other appropriate committee of the employee's organization will back the board and the administration in some flagrant cases when they reflect adversely on their own professionalism. In some situations legal counsel is willing to proceed if given the go-ahead sign when administrators prefer to do nothing.

The summary to this discussion is to urge you to analyze your own district carefully. Maybe you should do nothing about dismissals.

In the right situations and conditions, maybe you should have the guts to dismiss known incompetent employees. Even if you fail, the board and probably most of the staff and community will respect you more.

A good rule to follow is always to endeavor to help an employee before you dismiss him or her.

CITIZENS CAN TEACH, TOO

Many highly capable specialists in your district would welcome the opportunity to speak to a class or group regarding their speciality. Of course others would not be interested in the least and would decline. Such talks or demonstrations are not to be used as entertainment but as a part of the planned curriculum. The florist may have much to offer a botany class. Other examples of lay teachers are the TV repairman for a physics class, the city librarian for an English class, a computer expert for a math class, a retired traveler with his slides on Egypt or Rome for a history class, and professional football or basketball players for a P.E. class.

In an elementary school, a retired railroader or an airplane pilot may have a message for a class studying transportation. An adult who has developed a hobby on American Indians, the Aztecs, or Mayans may have films and other materials to present. A fireman or policeman can assist in a unit on the community.

Field trips within the community, particularly for primary students may include the water department, city library, museum, hospital, local court, fire station, police

office, a computer center, a nursery, garbage
collecting center, sewer department, and
health department.

The prime purpose of any of the above
is to improve instruction. But a valuable by-
product, if handled carefully, is community
involvement and improved public relations.

It is a worthwhile project for a graduate
student (possibly one of your own teachers)
to research and record data for the points
above in your own district.

ONE HUNDRED TIMES AND YOU ARE OUT

Twenty years ago an actor (friend of one
of the authors) played the part of Jesus in a
movie and for publicity purposes was advised
to have a scene in a hotel room involving the
actress playing the part of the sinful woman
of Samaria the night before the grand opening.
The theory was "any publicity is good publicity" regardless of the type. We are pleased
to report he said, "No."

A superintendent in the same community
for forty years at retirement said his name
had appeared in the local paper less than
one hundred times as a result of deliberate
action on his part. Nearly always he issued
all news releases for the district in the name
of the president of the board, a principal, the
head of athletics, the drama or music teacher,
but seldom as the school superintendent. He
said, "I always figured people get tired of
seeing public officials' names in the news
constantly. I decided I probably would get
fired after my name appeared in the paper

154

one hundred times, so I went out of the way
to stay under that figure. Maybe my apparent
success in this wealthy, suburban community
was due to other reasons, but I am firmly
convinced one very important factor was a
strict limitation of hogging the lime light,
giving credit to others, and keeping my name
out of the headlines."

Probably if you stopped ten people on
the street and asked them the name of your
school superintendent, seven would say they
did not know but hopefully they would add,
"He must be a good one for we sure have fine
schools." Maybe this represents a radical
point of view, but the authors believe it has
far more than a grain of truth.

At least compromise with us and avoid
too much publicity.

EVALUATE THE SUPERINTENDENT

In many districts all school employees
are evaluated except the superintendent. For
his own protection, he too should be evaluated.
Once a year on prepared forms each board
member should rate anonymously the various
factors listed and he or she should be able
to add comments. In situations of sharp
controversy and dissension maybe all ratings
should be collected and summarized by the
president of the board, a CPA, a judge, or a
trusted prominent citizen. If all can be
frank and honest, it is even better for the
evaluating to be done orally and face to face
in executive session. Each year in conference
with the superintendent the board should
determine major objectives they want him to
endeavor to meet. Maybe he is working extra

155

hard on the wrong things as far as the board
is concerned, and he does not learn this until
it is too late.

For your own protection as a superintendent insist on being evaluated. The summarized evaluation should be known by the entire
board and the superintendent. The new
objectives for the ensuing year should be
developed immediately after the evaluation is
presented.

EVALUATE THE BOARD?

One well known and successful superintendent evaluates each school board member
each year after he, the superintendent, is
evaluated by the board. He very frankly tells
one board member that he is dealing with school
employees instead of observing channels of
communication. Another is told he should find
a way to attend board meetings or resign. A
third member is urged to refrain in board
meetings from "playing up so much to the
audience." Advice, in a spirit of friendship is given to all as needed.

Many superintendents could do this and
get away with it and improve board relations
in doing it. Others are of such a personality
it would not work and the way they would
handle it would no doubt lead to their
dismissal.

The idea is good. Whether or not in your
situation you should try it, we leave to you.

- - -

*Outstanding administrators do great things
with little effort. Most of us must compensate
and do little things with great effort!*

CONTINGENCY PLANS

All personnel and students usually know what to do in case of fire, earthquake, or disaster and are drilled regularly for such events.

Sometimes the answers to the following are forgotten. May we ask what would be done in your district or school if:

1. The electricity goes off and the bell system in the schools does not work.

2. Four bus drivers call in sick at 6:00 a.m. and you have only two substitute bus drivers.

3. Three buses are vandalized during the night.

4. Electricity is off during the week-end and all frozen food for the cafeterias is spoiled.

5. One wing of a school building is destroyed by fire during the night, or an entire building is unusable because of vandalism.

6. One hour after lunch 200 children are suffering from food poisoning.

7. At the high school, students call a strike during the noon hour and refuse to return to classes.

8. Racial tension rises and gang fights take place during the school day.

"Now, what would you do if you found a ten foot
 snake in the hall?"

"Wow! I'd swear off drinking!"

9. Sewer lines become clogged at 10 a.m. on a school day, or due to a broken line an entire school plant is without water.

It is better to "borrow trouble" and know ahead of time what will be done for each of the above (and the many other situations you can list) rather than to attempt to come up with the best answer at the time of the crisis without previous planning.

These points are considered further under the heading of "Have a Back-Up Plan" in Part I.

P.E.R.T. AND GETTING READY

FOR A BOND ISSUE

P.E.R.T. (Program, Evaluation, Review, Technique) has application not only for the aerospace industry but also for school administration. Space does not permit an explanation of P.E.R.T. here and it is assumed the reader already knows it or will now learn about it.

It is particularly useful in conducting a bond election and the following represents one possible procedure. It all begins with a problem: Apparently new school building construction is needed.

A person (or committee) No. 1 is to make enrollment projections within three months for five years, ten years, and also at saturation using a specialist in this area.

Another person (or committee) No. 2 begins work on a master building plan for the district and relies on data to be received from No. 1.

Person (or committee) No. 3 makes preliminary analysis of existing sites and
availability of new sites, but waits for
report of No. 2 before making a preliminary
report.

The architect (No. 4) is employed at a
stipulated fee for preliminary assistance
but not for construction unless the bond issue
passes.

A person (or committee) No. 5 working
with all the above determines costs. Possibly
at this point the superintendent arranges for
an entire board meeting to be devoted to the
hearing of the above reports. Perhaps the
five reports are consolidated into one
"Summary Report" for the board.

An overall citizens committee is then
appointed by the board to hear facts and
results of the reports of the committee
reports. This new committee, in contrast to
previous ones should be large and a complete
cross-section of the community and its
organizations. It should include the good
guys and the bad guys and also appropriate
representation from the aforementioned
committees. If the overall citizens committee
seems favorable to further action, then a
date should be set for another meeting 30
days later. The 30 days allows representatives
of the various organizations to meet with
their respective groups or boards of directors
for instructions.

Hopefully the committee's report will
endorse strongly a bond issue of shall we
say, $5,000,000 which the business manager
computes can be handled by 20 year bonds at
an increase in the tax rate of 18¢ at first

but declining each year thereafter.

If the citizens committee is not willing to sponsor and/or endorse the bond issue, it will probably be best to wait awhile. A defeat is more than loss of a bond issue; it is a defeat for the administration, for the board, and for the schools.

P.E.R.T. AND THE BOND CAMPAIGN

It is assumed as a result of the Community Committee Report considered in the previous topic, the news release on the first page of the local paper will read, "Citizens Demand School Bond Issue." The subhead will read, "Board Calls Bond Issue--Asks for Community Support."

Now is the time to use P.E.R.T. again. The entire procedure for the bond campaign should now be diagrammed (charted) by use of lines that meet, diverge, and meet again.

One line will represent the "publicity committee," another the "get out the favorable vote committee," another the lay speakers' bureau, and other committees as needed in various situations.

One committee will be in charge of selecting a captain (precinct worker) for each block in the school district. This committee will determine by house to house canvass who are probable "yes" votes and who are sure "no" votes and those who are "undecided." Thus concentration later can be made on the "undecided" and the "yes" voters. The probably "no" votes are ignored.

161

A campaign fund and expense committee
will be included and shown on the chart.
At various points these lines and others
(as information is interchanged) will meet
and separate on charts and meet again but all
will converge at the end.

The campaign activities including the
telephone calls the night before the election, poll-list watching on election day,
baby-sitting for voters and transportation for
voters as needed will be included in the
overall P.E.R.T. program.

One community known to the authors has
never lost a bond or tax election. P.E.R.T.
was used. However, the superintendents have
said that the keys to their success are:
(1) avoid mass publicity and large meetings,
(2) have an administrator meet with representatives of every civic, religious, business,
and fraternal organization in the community to
secure a favorable resolution of approval,
(3) have dozens of "coffee clatches" where
not more than 10 people gather in a home to
hear an administrator give facts and elicit
help with the neighbors, (4) leave "no" votes
alone, (5) schedule the election as a special
election rather than combined with a state or
national election, (6) avoid threats and fear
tactics, (7) start the campaign not more than
six weeks prior to the election, (8) the day
before the election have committee workers
telephone potential "yes" voters and remind
them to vote.

Following the successful bond election
the committees will be honored, thanked and
each member will be given a "Sidewalk
Building Superintendent's Card."

The remaining jobs of selling bonds, site acquisitions, contracts, change orders, and supervision are all administrative functions and should be handled by administrators (with school board approval) and not by committees--the worst form of administration. However, these administrative duties and time lines will be outlined by use of P.E.R.T.

Possibly the reader has used P.E.R.T. for various tasks at least in his mind already. We hope he will use it on a formalized basis for many functions to be performed over a period of time. It has effectiveness when used for tax elections, budget development, curriculum development, and maintenance projects, personnel procedures and other areas.

WHO IS YOUR NEGOTIATOR?

School employees are no longer docile. We have strong employee organizations, employees may strike whether it is legal or not, and even in most of the best situations the administration can expect many hours of negotiating starting off with unreasonable demands with the employees hoping to get half of what was demanded.

One outstanding city superintendent remarked to us, "I did the very best I could for the teachers--got them almost as much as they demanded, but they are very unhappy with me. In pressing the board for the raise, the board felt that after all these 25 years I had sold out to the teachers. Thus I lost the board and the teachers. You cannot win. I'm taking an early retirement and calling it quits."

Techniques used against you are to make
you angry so you will regret what you say;
use so much of your time you reach exaspera-
tion or the breaking point; to divide your
board; or to divide you and the board; dis-
credit you with the community; or have a
"sick-in" if not a strike.

In 90 percent of the districts the board
and you will both come out ahead if you employ
an outside negotiator or firm to handle the
bulk of the negotiating process. It's almost
impossible to be a professional leader as well
as a negotiator at the same time.

To push negotiating off on one of your
assistant superintendents (personnel or
business) is not the answer. In some ways
it is worse than if you, the superintendent,
do it. Their specific areas involving business,
legal, and personnel problems won't wait for
negotiating to cease.

Check with other superintendents who
have used professional negotiators and see if
they don't agree with the above. You, the
superintendent, should not be the chief
negotiator. A fine job you do for the district will probably result in poorer relations
with employees on matters other than salaries
if you become the antagonist.

- - -

*If possible, you should schedule or provide
for yourself some "alone" time each day and use
this for quiet meditation, introspection, and
creating a feeling of inner peace. It is so
easy as an administrator to become buried or
engulfed by other people.*

PART IV

PERSONAL QUALITIES

165

I cannot hear what he says, for I might
miss what he does next!

PERSONAL IRRITANTS

     Bill Crude is the Director of Curric-
ulum in the High Culture Unified School
District. He has a doctorate, excellent
experience in his field and nearly always
makes the right decisions. Yet Bill does
does not get his points across in staff
meetings. His nervous little habits gain
the attention of listeners rather than what
he is saying. Staff members conducted 10¢
bets regarding which habit he would exhibit
first after all were seated and which one
he would do most often during the meeting.

     The carefully kept tallies during each
meeting included: tapping his fingers on
the table, adjusting his tie, jingling
change in his pocket, twirling the small
knife on the end of his watch chain,
saying "all right" at the end of each
point made, picking at his nose, adjusting
his glasses, pulling up his pants, inspect-
ing his fingernails, cleaning his glasses,
routinely looking up at ceiling while
talking, running a hand through his hair,
picking up papers in front of himself and
restacking them for no reason, moving
keys around on his key chain, clipping
fingernails with pocket clippers, repeating
"you know" over and over, wiping forehead
with handkerchief, or buttoning his coat
and then rebuttoning it.

     All of us let off nervous tension by
using some little quirk that in itself is
inconsequential, but such habits are an
annoyance and an irritant to others. They
will weaken administrative effectiveness.

167

Probably your best friends will not volunteer to tell you, so: (1) do a good job of introspection, (2) insist a close friend tell you what bad habits you have picked up, and (3) at the end of a meeting insist that everyone write a one sentence suggestion to be compiled anonymously by another person. Then work to eliminate these personal irritants.

YOUR BOSS IS A FOOL

You are in the barber shop and several fellows are really taking your boss apart and they turn to you and ask, "What do you think of him?"

One school of thought says you defend him right or wrong--you are always loyal. Another says don't say anything, but silence probably will be interpreted as assent. There is no final, absolute answer for all situations.

In general, we would say if the boss is right or even close to right (as you see it), you should defend him even though you know it is not the popular thing to do.

If the boss is really wrong (as you see it) and he has made a fool of himself, the least you can do is to say, "Listen fellows, he's my boss who helps decide my salary and whether I'm hired or fired. You wouldn't respect me if I criticized him-- let's talk about something else."

In other situations where the boss is being justly criticized, you can at least point out, "Regardless of what you're

MY BOSS IS GREAT!

saying, we have to admit he is . . . ."
The rest of the sentence is some good
quality or stand he has taken that is
recognized by those present.

In brief, we stay loyal and defend
the boss if at all possible. Under no
condition do we criticize him. As a last
resort, even though he is dead wrong, we
use one of the two alternatives mentioned.

MR. BANOWSKY CAN HELP YOU

An able young principal, Maylon Drake,
applied for his first superintendency in a
neighboring town. Competition was keen as
there were 76 applicants. Finally the
principal was appointed; he and his wife
were thrilled; and they lived happily ever
after.

Six months after being appointed everything was going fine and the new superintendent asked the president of the school
board just why he was chosen when there
were so many others with fine recommendations and qualifications. The board president told him that the board had checked
with his superintendent, members of the
school board, the local newspaper editor,
and the town banker. All had given him
good reports, but the clincher was the
report given by Mr. Banowsky.

Now, Mr. Banowsky was the head custodian at Drake's previous school. Mr.
Banowsky had said, "I hope you don't hire
him. He's the best principal you could ever
know. He is liked by the kids, teachers,
and parents. We classified folks think he

is great--he is not stuck up, treats us as equals, and is a regular guy. Furthermore, he runs a darn good school and I'm glad to have my two kids in it."

The board president said Mr. Banowsky's remarks had meant more to him than all the others put together and, "if you want to thank someone--thank Mr. Banowsky." Hopefully your classified employees will like you and say good things about you because you like and respect them. Even if such is not the case, it would be good personal politics to have Mr. Banowsky on your side. Too many administrators would not even know the Mr. Banowsky in their school districts.

(This point is considered further in Part I under heading of "Be Sure To Visit the Custodian.")

STEAL A MILLION DOLLARS

A metropolitan newspaper reported a few years ago in the same issue these two stories: A black man stole $150 (excess of $100 was a felony) and received a ten-year sentence. A wealthy financeer embezzled $1,000,000 and received a two-year sentence and was paroled for good behavior at the end of one year. The moral developed on an unjustified basis would seem to be if you are going to steal, then take at least a million dollars--and don't be a member of a minority group or a poor person!

You steal the pencil--I'm taking a
million dollars!

The authors can name the persons, dates, and places of the following. One superintendent was released (resigned) for using school stamps to pay his personal monthly bills. Another administrator was dismissed for using the school district telephone to call her parents out of state each Sunday night. Another took exactly $10 a day from cafeteria funds for two years and was then caught.

If and when you are fired, it probably will not be for some big thing but for a lot of little points. If we came to your home tonight, would we observe school pencils, thumb tacks, paperclips, rubber bands, and school stamps? Using personal money for school business and then paying yourself back with the items mentioned is still wrong and illegal.

If you are going to steal, take a million dollars, but don't let others lose confidence in you by noting you are guilty of minor pilfering. The value of this small stuff during your lifetime as an administrator will probably be worth less than $500. Even if your conscience does not bother you, play it smart.

– – –

There is no place for use of sarcasm on the job, with your wife or children. Delete sarcasm completely as an instrument of correction or rebuke.

THE LITTLE THINGS

Ben Franklin said, "A small leak will
sink a great ship." He might have added
school administrators become unacceptable
in a community because they are so
absorbed in the big things they forget the
little things that will make or break them.

And don't you forget the little things!

An administrator is not paying attention to the little things when he becomes
absorbed in his own thoughts and passes
people without speaking; barges through a
door hurriedly and lets it swing back in
the face of another; is so busy he doesn't
have time to let a person finish a sentence
before he interrupts; always arrives at
functions late; when introduced to others
responds mechanically without feeling or
answers with a trite expression; does not
work at remembering names and others feel
insulted after several such instances; keeps
telling how busy he is; talks about self
rather than about matters of interest to
others; or neglects the wives of others at
a social affair.

An elementary music supervisor directed
the play "The House That Jack Built" and
it was such a success it had to be repeated
two additional nights. It was probably one
of the finest productions ever presented by
an elementary school (K-8). She was
applauded for the outstanding performances,
but at the end of the school year, she was
released (before the days of tenure laws).
She had forgotten the little things and had
concentrated only on the one big thing--the
play. Preparatory to the presentation she
berated custodians, had parents in tears
because costumes were not quite right,
angered the entire staff by taking students
out of classes for rehearsals, and upset
the bus schedules and cafeteria noon program
by continuing rehearsals longer than agreed.

It was the old story of winning the
battle but losing the war, or being unable
to see the forest for the trees.

When you are involved in a big project,
remember to force yourself to give extra
attention to the little things. This
includes husband or wife when you get home,
tired and irritable.

HOW CLUTTERED IS THE TOP OF YOUR DESK?

An administrator is judged not only by a
ring around the collar, unshined shoes, and
baggy pants, but also by the top of his desk.
The top right hand drawer can be used for
"urgent items," the second drawer for "not
so urgent," another one for "no hurry,"
and one other for third class mail. To
have similar stacks on top of the desk is
observed frequently and much shuffling of
papers to find a needed document takes place.

A cluttered desk does not show you are
real busy, a hard worker, a very important
person, or that you are over-worked and
should get a raise. It does show that you
are disorganized; you don't keep things
moving; you are a poor housekeeper; you
probably have other sloppy habits; you are
a procrastinator; a lot of things come to
your desk that should never come there in
the first place; you are bogged down in
trivia; and you don't know how to delegate.
Even if you are guilty of some of these, hide
the evidence in the drawers of your desk.

You can tell a lot about an administrator
by observing the top of his desk or going to
his home and observing how he arranges his
socks, handkerchiefs, underwear, shoes, and
pajamas in dresser drawers or closets.

Let's see. . . where did I file that?

Urge all employees to leave a clean
desk each night. If you cannot find time
to get rid of the stacks on your own desk,
you might just throw it all away--it
probably won't make much difference in
most cases anyway!

177

You have observed many "I am the most humble man I have ever known" superintendents who treat board members and civic leaders as superiors. They give the impression they are always "trying to butter them up," or "get in good with them," or "be a yes man" so as to keep job security by appearing humble and subservient.

You also have observed the school principal who is now out of the classroom and "talks down" to people as he did to his pupils when he was a teacher. But a good teacher does not talk down to his or her pupils. Talking down includes repeating the same statement for emphasis, explaining things in great detail, correcting people, tone of voice used, endeavoring to win an argument, interrupting others or sighing in replying to a question. It includes expressions of "Let me tell you," and "One thing I know for sure is . . . ."

It is not always what you say but how you say it and how loudly and emphatically. It includes making the other person ill at ease or asking questions the other person has to keep answering, "I don't know."

There is a middle ground which involves showing genuine interest, concern, courtesy, and respect but avoids subserviency. It includes doing small favors for others but

178

not of magnitude involving obligation;
being friendly but not over solicitous;
and "doing unto others as you . . . . "

    Don't talk up--don't talk down. Talk
across, friendly and courteously, and as to
equals in nearly all cases.

A soft answer turns away wrath, but grievous
words stir up anger. The more angry the
other person becomes, the good administra-
tor, in general, becomes calmer and lowers
his voice

- - -

CAPITALIZE ON YOUR WEAKNESS

Joe E. Brown made a fortune off his
big mouth. Jimmie Snozzle Durante did likewise with his large nose. Ben Turpin
capitalized on his crossed eyes. The TV
detective, Cannon, joked about his being fat.
Laurel and Hardy made the most of being big
and little.

If you have a bald head, then collect
bald-headed stories and tell them on yourself. If because of your race or nation-
ality, your speech is different from others,
instead of trying to cover up, develop
jokes to tell in your own dialect. If you
are too thin, fat, little, big, or have
just one arm, then joke about it. A man
with a wooden leg should have a story about
the termites bothering him. A man with new
false teeth giving him trouble should tell
about how he was bit when he sat down while
dressing and sat on his false teeth. If
your drawl locates you as having come from
the South, you have a warehouse full of
stories about the Southern gentleman,
Scarlet O'Hara, the Confederacy, or the
Mississippi River gambler.

We are all different--some a little
more so than others. If you are different,
don't develop an inferiority complex, try to

cover up or even ignore it. Instead, bring it out in the open and capitalize on it by use of good humor on your difference--they need not be weaknesses. Make them into strengths.

I guess I goofed--yes I did goof! Now to face the music.

YES, I GOOFED

We all know if we demand that our own children tell us the truth about a mistake they have made and then when they do, we in turn punish them severely, we are encouraging them to become liars.

George Washington, if he chopped down the cherry tree, confessed, and said he could not tell a lie was absolutely right in admitting he goofed. We trust the punishment, if any, was clearly lessened because he told the truth.

If the principal makes a mistake in reporting the number of accidents on the playground for the past month, we hope when he learns it he will admit he goofed, rather than blaming his secretary (she may have caused it) or covering it up by telling half truths. We hope the superintendent will respond to the principal by saying, "Thanks for telling me. No great harm has been done—and I feel better than ever for I now know you'll never do that again." Helping the one who made a mistake save face (embarrassment or humiliation) is just as important as it is for the one who made it to admit it freely.

Since you as an administrator are responsible for mistakes of your subordinates, accept the blame and don't even tell who really caused it. The public has a warmer feeling for a superintendent who states in the paper regarding some mix-up that received adverse publicity: "I accept full responsibility for this since I am in

182

charge. We are very sorry and will do our
best to see it does not happen again."

- - -

The accused has a right to face his accusor--
which applies also to administrators in
dealing with employees

- - -

O WAD SOME POWER THE GIFTIE GIE US

Robert Burns wrote:

> *O Wad Some Power the giftie gie us*
> *To see oursels as others see us.*
> *It wad frae mony a blunder free us,*
> *An foolish notion.*

Our personality is not how we see ourselves but how others see us. I may visualize
myself as modest, conservative, and calm.
Others may see me as an egoist, liberal,
and nervous, which then is what I really am
for all practical purposes. Sensitivity
groups will let you see yourself as others
do but they can be brutal and dangerous;
and unless handled by a genuine expert,
will do more harm than good.

A safer approach is to do some honest
introspection for five minutes each day when
all is quiet and you are alone. A spouse
can help if he or she does not overreact in
making suggestions and you overreact in
receiving them. A close friend or colleague
may do the job even better.

A professor insisted at the end of a graduate course in administration that each student write one anonymous sentence as a suggestion for his improvement. He received so much help he has repeated it once a year ever since, but he says it "really shakes me up for two or three days each time."

One of his (or your) strengths may be a trait not always acceptable, but it might be a shame to alter a uniqueness that has proven successful thus far.

Try some serious and honest introspection for a few minutes each day. See if it doesn't help; for none of us is perfect.

THE INDIVIDUAL LOST IN THE GROUP

In a group situation are you talking to the group of fifteen or to fifteen individuals? We hope it is the latter. Then you will be your natural self, you will not orate or sermonize, and you will not button your vest and adjust your tie just as you begin. What you say and how you say it will be different if you are just talking to individuals. All groups are made up of individuals. See individuals in the group as you talk. We hope your teachers in dealing with their classes do this, too.

- - -

Abraham Lincoln described character like a tree and reputation like its shadow. The shadow is what we think of; the tree is the real thing.

THE SCHOOLTEACHER IN YOU IS SHOWING

"When I went to school early this morning, I found it a wreck. Vandals had broken in over the weekend and had turned on the fire house in the hall. There were about two inches of water everywhere. In the cafeteria about twenty dishes had been thrown against the wall. Catsup was squirted all over the tables and five windows were broken and glass was all around. Believe me it was a mess."

"Yes, would you believe when I arrived at school this morning there were two inches of water coming from the fire hose down the hall floor into the cafeteria. In the cafeteria I saw twenty or more dishes which had been broken by the vandals throwing them against the wall-- catsup was spread all over the tables, and five windows were broken with glass all over the floor. You should have seen it. It was the worse mess I've seen."

The schoolteacher in us sometimes says the same thing twice (hopefully in a different way) in a classroom for emphasis and to make sure the slow learner gets the point the second time around.

For us adults to repeat a point to another adult is "talking down to him" or would seem to indicate we don't think he is very intelligent. Probably it is meant to be neither--we have developed just a very bad habit of saying the same thing twice, particularly when we are a little nervous or ill at ease.

The moral is: Say it just once, just once, just once!

It was a mess!

It, was a mess.

It was--a mess!

186

EXPRESSIONS TO AVOID

If you are using any of the following, work to eliminate them as soon as possible:

1. "May I have just a minute"--then take 30 minutes.

2. "Now this is the truth"--implies what you said before was not.

3. "This is highly confidential but I'll tell you"--better not tell it.

4. "You will have to go down the hall and enter the last office on the right"--people resent being told they "have to"; instead, say, "It is the last office on the right."

5. "Just between you and me"--implies favoritism.

6. "That's a good question"--implies others were not.

7. "You cannot miss it"--and most do.

8. "Don't blame me, I just work here"--shows disloyalty.

9. "I'm sorry, the board ordered that"--again is not loyal.

10. "Our hick town"--be proud of it or move to another.

11. "I am going to"--we are endeavoring to.

12. "My schools are"--our schools are.

187

13. "Now let me tell you"--dogmatic and egotistic.

14. "I just cannot believe it!"--trite or indicates the other person is a liar.

15. "Those Mexicans"--local situation will be Latin-Americans, Mexican-Americans, or even Chicanos, but seldom Mexicans.

16. "Colored people"--blacks, maybe Negroes. Use blacks with whites and Caucasian with Negro, and when possible be colorblind and avoid terms of blacks, whites, and Mexican-Americans.

17. "Those non-certificated"--classified, and not non-professional either.

18. "Etc."--go ahead and say what the "and so forth" is but don't leave us wondering what the "etc." is.

19. "I just died when I heard it"--shall we call the funeral director?

20. "It's fantastic"--if you heard Marv's "fantastic" joke, you will not use the word "fantastic" again.

21. "Have a good day"--is used so much now it has little meaning. Use some of the many other expressions such as: "It was a pleasure to visit with you." "I hope I will see you again soon." "Come back anytime."

22. "You know"--to start nearly every sentence. We "know" that you are tired of hearing "you know" repeatedly.

SO YOUR NAME IS BOB

As the new principal or superintendent you
will have to decide the first day who you are.
Are you "Bob"- Are you Dr. Ferris"- Are you
Mr. Ferris?" The answer is situational and
depends on your own personality and on past
and current expectations of the community.

A young administrator who had just received
his doctorate was appointed to the position of
Assistant Director of Operations in the business
division of a large city district. The director,
an able man, was just a high school graduate.
Our young administrator wisely chose to be "Mr."
instead of "Dr." In his next position he was
requested to be "Dr." as his having a doctorate
degree was one reason he was selected.

A few miles apart two neighboring superintendents made different choices and apparently
both were right. In the first, the board was
proud to have its superintendent to be "Doctor
Walter Adams" and the community was the type
where the citizens agreed.

In the other district past custom was for
the superintendent just to be one of the boys
and "Dr. Robert E. Ferris" would have served as
an unnecessary barrier. When he said, "Just
call me Bob," it was a very smart move.

"Bob" in some places would lower your
prestige and dignity. "Dr. Ferris" in others
would make you a "starched shirt and a city guy
who is not one of us."

Probably you should stay whatever you
already are in your present community.

If there is a move to another community, make
the choice instead of just letting it happen.
Even if you choose not to use "Doctor,"
never disparage your degree in an effort
toward modesty. No one will respect you for
that.

GOOD GUYS AND BAD GUYS

Ten percent of us are probably really
"good guys" and ten percent are probably "bad
guys." The other 80 percent of us are not
wearing a white hat nor a black hat, but instead
a gray one. One of the worst habits we can get
into is to classify people as "good" or "bad"
as it will show in our subconscious actions.
Most things are not just black, nor white, but
are gray; not yes or no, but maybe; not hot or
cold but medium; not tall or short, but average;
and neither heroes nor villains, but just
ordinary folks.

There is some bad in the best of us and a
lot of good in the worst of us. Deal with
people not only on a "colorblind basis" but also
on a "not good or bad guy" basis. Showing
prejudice or favoritism for Catholics, Jews, or
Protestants; for Democrats or Republicans; for
black, brown, or white; for the affluent or poor;
or for good guys and bad guys is a common
mistake.

See the good in the worst of people and
capitalize on their good points using them freely
where their strong points apply. Avoid using the
good guy exclusively or in a situation where his
limitations will weaken his influence. Whenever possible compliment the bad guy for his
good points. The town drunk may be a good
whittler, the anti-school taxpayer may be a good
whistler, and the card shark and gambler may be
just the right one to help organize the
Halloween Carnival.

Remember the bad guys have a vote on bond
issues and tax elections the same as the good

Are you one of the _bad guys_?

192

guys. Why alienate anyone? It is a luxury
we cannot afford. There should be no such thing
as good and bad guys. They are all people.
Some have certain qualities we like or dislike,
but we must learn to live with everyone.

ALL CARDS ON TOP OF THE TABLE

A compliment is paid you when those who do
not agree with you volunteer, "Well, he at least
keeps all his cards on top of the table."

People will not respect you if they suspect
you of double dealing, keeping a card up your
sleeve, or dealing off the bottom of the deck.
Perhaps we had better add that we realize school
administration is not a game of poker nor is it
trying to outsmart others. But good school
administration does include telling the whole
truth instead of half-truths, admitting you are
wrong when you are wrong, and answering a
question directly, possibly adding, "I believe
you are trying to get more information con-
cerning. . . . If such is the case, I will be
glad to give you some additional facts, though
I am not very proud of them."

A good school administrator excludes working
through fear, keeping people off-balance, being
evasive, or outsmarting another by improper use
of semantics. The good school administrator is
open and above board; he tells the truth even
when it hurts; and he is honest and frank.
He keeps all cards on top of the table even
though he doesn't play poker.

- - -

*Learn to observe and read a person's body
language for good clues to reactions.*

193

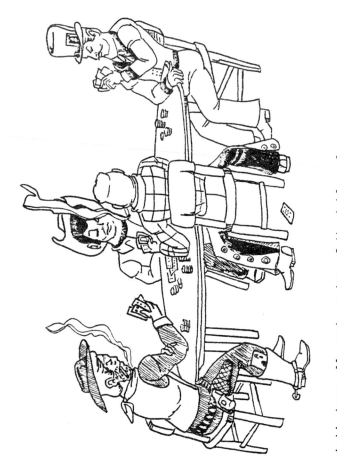

Let's have all cards on top of the table, please.

We hope your spouse is attractive, sincerely friendly with everyone, and a strong backer of you, the administrator. We hope he or she does not correct you or argue with you in public, but that such points are settled in privacy at home. We trust he or she is genuinely interested in the schools and community and will accept assignments for PTA, Red Cross, Community Chest (other than soliciting money), Girl Scouts, local service clubs, and other fine organizations. We hope that he or she does not endeavor to dominate any of them or as a rule become president.

We hope your spouse has some personal interests and hobbies such as golf, art, music, or bridge which are not related to the schools or your activities. We trust he or she is an extrovert rather than an introvert, an optimist and not a pessimist, a doer rather than just a receiver.

We hope he or she can keep a closed mouth regarding school affairs and gossip. We trust that your spouse is a good listener rather than an avid talker.

We believe in Women's Lib and if she is an administrator (and we need more women as administrators), then all this advice applies to the husband. He must not be the royal knight rushing around to defend the fair lady, his wife, but realize she must defend herself if she accepts an administrative position of public leadership.

195

WHO CARES?

One well known administrator each time he
met a person he had not seen in several days
always began the conversation with, "How is
your lovely wife? How are those two fine boys
(or girls)? And you're fine, I assume?" Usually
he did not wait for one answer until he asked
the next question. This soon became a community joke that hurt him in the eyes of others.
It is easy to develop stereotyped forms of
greetings.

One of the authors whose office was on the
ninth floor of the School of Education building
conducted an unscientific experiment five
consecutive mornings. Since the professor had
been at the university for more than 25 years,
he was known by most of the students and secretaries using the elevator. Typically each
morning several of the elevator occupants would
greet him with a "Good morning" and at least
one would say routinely, "How are you today?"

The experiment consisted of the professor
smiling broadly and in a very cheerful tone of
voice answered, "Very badly, I think I am dying
and How Are You?" Three days of the five days
the answer was, "Just fine, thank you" as the
professor's answer was not noticed.

People appreciate being recognized, spoken
to and generally are pleased you are interested
enough to inquire about them. It is spoiled,
however, when it becomes obvious you don't
even hear their reply and the whole thing is
a routine without meaning. If you are really
interested and intend to listen to the reply,
ask. Otherwise, forget it and just say,
"Good morning!"

At the end of a three-table bridge party attended by two school teachers, dessert was served and one large group conversation ensued. Unfortunately the teachers started talking about "school" which was not an exciting conversation topic for the others. The conversation then centered on Max Fergus who was suspended that day for fighting. Then one of the teachers remarked, "What can you expect-- his I.Q. is only 85, his dad chases women, and his mother stays half-drunk all day."

No banker would have made such a (or any) comment about one of his depositors, nor a doctor about one of his patients. Teachers should forget school at social functions and under no circumstance give privileged information to others.

To avoid a suit for slander, there should be the following components: (1) There should be inquiry by a person privileged to know (police officer, welfare worker, or those stipulated in the state law). (2) There should be no malice ("I wouldn't recommend him for dog catcher" shows malice). (3) There is no protection in repeating what someone else said, and (4) Check again to make sure the inquirer is privileged to know what you are being asked to tell.

Educators will never achieve professional status so long as they indulge in idle gossip. A teacher has privileged communication to the principal, the principal has it to the superintendent, and the superintendent to the school board, but none of these has privileged

197

communication at a bridge party.

Think about it. How much do you talk about school, away from school?

I am awarding the plaintiff $10,000. You talked too much!

WE DID IT THIS WAY IN OKLAHOMA

A preacher, Bob Jones, in Texas quoted his home state of Oklahoma in glowing terms so often in his sermons that on one occasion one of the good sisters said, "Parson, I have a real problem--I just cannot make up my mind when I die whether I would rather go to heaven or to Oklahoma."

If you are from Oklahoma but now work in California, forget Oklahoma even though your going to California raised the I.Q. average of both states. People just are not interested in how it was done in Oklahoma. Don't orate on the virtues of another place to the point that the people wish you would go back there.

The same is true if you constantly quote your previous experiences in another school district in the same state.

The same point applies to quoting the good old days when you were a student in school. Living in the past makes no one respect you. Gone are the days of crew haircuts for boys, and gingham dresses for girls. Gone are the days when you say, "The reason you do it is because I said so," or "When I say jump, you try even though you have a broken leg."

Oklahoma (unless you live in that great state) is far away. Yesterday is gone forever-- likewise the good old days. You are living now where you are and for today and tomorrow. Even more certain than taxes is "change." Don't fight it!

Good Lord, PLEASE make heaven just like Oklahoma!

I'LL NEVER FORGET EMMA B. EBY

It was my first year as a small-town superintendent. My predecessor was Emma B. Eby who had been the superintendent in the district "forever" according to the oldtimers. She was age 65, had snow white hair, and had been a great Christian woman, an educational leader, a skilled administrator, and one loved by the grandmothers, the mothers, and the children for she had taught them all.

After she retired and I had accepted the position, she asked the board if she could stay on just one more year as an eighth grade teacher. The request was granted with enthusiasm.

I was greatly concerned. I now would have the "just short of God and previous superintendent" looking over my shoulder while I was learning to be a superintendent. A man was never more wrong. She was supportive in every way and I learned many things from her that were not in the textbooks on school administration.

The point I appreciated most was "never speak evil of anyone," and she practiced it! She was never heard to criticize any one. When a girl in her room came to school severely beaten by her drunken father, I denounced him as a "drunken old fool" to Mrs. Eby in a loud voice. Her reply was, "He's pretty sharp and a long ways from being a fool. He is the 'good old man' who leveled our playground free of charge a few years ago." She then went to the girl and said, "Come on, Honey, let's go see if the school nurse can help you while he watches my class. We'll be back soon." I "watched" her class.

201

Emma B. Eby never criticized anyone and
everyone loved her. It is not realistic for
you to never criticize anyone. You are paid
to do some of it in evaluating employees.
However, you are not paid to drop unnecessary
disparaging remarks. See if you can be as
good as old Mrs. Eby for just 24 hours and say
nothing bad about anyone unless the exception
you make is when the job demands it.

DO YOUR OWN THING

Dr. John Sexson, formerly Superintendent
of Pasadena, California, when it was a light-
house in public education, was one of the
greatest of public school administrators. His
many honors included the presidency of AASA.
Dr. Sexson "cussed" beautifully, sounding
more like soft music than profanity. He told
shady stories that made a point rather than
being just dirty. He was a gruff, loud spoken,
but a kind gentleman with a deep bass voice.

A promising young assistant, who admired
Dr. Sexson very much, imitated his voice, and
used Dr. Sexson's gruffness, profanity, and
shady stories. He got himself in all kinds of
trouble. What the boss in his sixties could
do and be acceptable was entirely different
from what a young assistant could do.

A cute, little 16 year old school girl
who puts on a false personality to become more
like her favorite movie star misses the boat
also.

Copying qualities of courtesy, friendliness,
optimism, and thoughtfulness will work and is
recommended. Imitating unique qualities of a
man like John Sexson will not.

202

"Parson, that was a damn good sermon against profanity--
so I put $50 in the plate!"

"The hell you say!"

Unless "doing your own thing" includes
crudeness, vulgarity, selfishness, egotism,
or unacceptable habits, you will come out ahead
to be your own natural self. You must not have
been too bad or you would not have reached
that point of success you have already achieved
in just being plain "you."

PROFANITY AND SHADY STORIES

This discussion is not concerned with the
religious or moral aspects of profanity. That
is a problem each individual must decide for
himself, but if you accept the Bible, then
read Deuteronomy 5:11 and Matthew 5:22-23.

No one has greater respect for you because
of your dirty speech and it does not make you
more of a "he-man" or "she-woman." So many
people object to it that it doesn't make good
political sense nor does it increase job security.
Yes, we can point to several outstanding administrators who "cuss like a sailor" and do it so
smoothly that it sounds like poetry. They are
the exception that proves the rule. For most of
us it shows a deficiency in our vocabulary, a
lack of culture and refinement, and an inability
to express ourselves adequately.

Telling stories regarding religion can
also be a real liability. Though a Jew, Catholic,
Protestant, black man, Italian, or Irish man or
women may love to tell stories on their own
people, they may not appreciate your doing the
same.

One of the authors was present when the
speaker talking to an audience of about 1,000
told the following story: "A Mormon had twenty

204

wives and each had a separate house a half-mile
apart covering 10 miles down the road. When he
wanted a different wife in the main house, he
sent his messenger for her. The Mormon lived
to the ripe old age of 105 but the messenger
died at age 25."

This was told with proper embellishment
to make it into a humorous story. At the end
of the story, a dignified man in the middle of
the audience rose and said in a loud but courteous
voice, "As a member of the Church of Jesus Christ
of Latter Day Saints I resent this story which
reflects adversely on my church." You could
have heard a pin drop. Fortunately, the speaker
apologized, thanked him, promised not to do it
again, and then continued with his speech. That
speaker never again told a shady story or one
relating to religion or race.

WANTED: A WEE BIT OF CULTURE

School administrators have "arrived" from
many different backgrounds, including the
popular coach, the Phi Beta Kappa chemistry
teacher, and the elementary modern math teacher
who has had more education courses than all
other courses combined. The above in no way
implies that the above are not all good administrators; in fact, let us assume that all three
of them are outstanding administrators.

However, the former coach may not know
whether Alexander the Great (356-323 BC) con-
quered much of Asia before or after Gengis
Khan (1162-1227AD). The Phi Beta Kappa chemistry
teacher may not know a Rembrandt from a Picasso.
The elementary math teacher may say, "Who did
he give it to?" or "The data is wrong," or "It
will be too late for you and I to go."

They said I need to acquire some culture.

When board members and local citizens expect us as educators to be "cultured" and we show weaknesses in an area where we should not, they tend to lose confidence in our administrative ability.

The former coach should take a high school history textbook (ancient, medieval, and modern) home and turn through it for two or three evenings instead of watching TV sport reports. The chemistry teacher needs to take home a textbook or just a paperback on the History of Art. The elementary teacher may need to study a freshman English text. All three may need a high school textbook on English Literature, American Literature, and a paperback on the History of Music.

Now is the time to think for a minute regarding weak areas in your background. Stay away from college textbooks. Culture yourself a wee bit with elementary and high school textbooks and encyclopedias for children.

Add a wee bit of culture where your slip is showing!

- - -

As we get older with our vast store of wisdom it seems a pity not to use it all. It takes strength not to say something on every subject and on every occasion and to try to straighten out everybody's affairs. Remember, we want a few friends at the end!

UNNECESSARY ADJECTIVES

Possibly you have heard a preacher at
church describe a person or situation using
four or five adjectives all meaning about the
same thing. It seems when he does this repeatedly and pauses a second or two to try to think
of an additional adjective to add that he is
making a strong effort to display his linquistic
abilities and command of the English language
rather than to save souls. You get lost by his
flowery speech in the point he is trying to make.
Since school administrators make many public
speeches, some have picked up this poor habit
and have joined the ranks of the preacher described. Don't do it!

Some of us are guilty of using adjectives
that really tell very little. Examples: He
has a big house, a large yard, an old neighbor-
hood, a small car, a lot of money, a house full
of kids, a pleasant wife, and a small dog.
We could say he has a ten-room house on an acre
of land, a VW car, he is worth $200,000 probably,
has five children, and a very charming and
pretty blonde wife.

Words should be used to communicate ideas
rather than conceal them.

We feel this point is terrific, collosal,
stupendous, fantastic, gigantic, and incredible--
also superior, excellent, and oustanding!

- - -

*Learning to read is as important for the school
administrator as for the child starting school--
especially reading for pleasure.*

208

A SENTENCE INSTEAD OF A PARAGRAPH

When asked a question, answer it and don't tell the story of your life in doing so. Probably all you need to say is "Yes," or "No," or "About 125," or "Tommorrow at 3 p.m.," or "his extension number is 0304."

Get to the point immediately; answer courteously and briefly. Possibly you should add, "May I help further?" We have made our point so we too will be brief and stop right here.

I <u>sentence</u> you to listen to the story of my life!

DON'T WEAR A TUX TO A BEACH PARTY

The authors have a policy of checking up
on newly placed school superintendents. After
three or four months, the president of the
school board of the new superintendent is con-
tacted. Recently at a convention the authors
asked about a number of new superintendents.
The reports on two are given here.

In the first case the president was
asked, "How is Dr. Joe Anonymous doing as your
new superintendent? We feel sure you will report
'fine' for he is a very able man but we just
want to be sure and give him any help if we
can."

The answer given by the first board member
was, "Joe is great and we thank you again for
recommending him to us. Only one little minor
point bothers us." When asked what this point
was, he replied: "He dresses as if he wears
a tuxedo to a beach party. He just plain over-
dresses for our farming community. His expensive suits, tailored shirts, gold cufflinks,
and diamond stickpins are just out of place
among us country folks."

And as you have no doubt guessed already,
the school board president from the second district gave an equally glowing report but the one
minor point bothering him was, "He doesn't dress
well enough for our sophisticated suburban
community and we pay him a good enough salary so he
certainly can afford some decent clothes.
Everything he wears is out of style and obviously
was bought at some cut-rate clothing store. Why
don't you fellows work him over a little?"

210

I figure if you own it, you should wear it!

In any situation the minister and the school administrator should be dressed as well or a little better than the average citizen of the community. Too far above or too far below the accepted standards of the community represents poor taste and judgment.

Are you wearing a tux to the beach party or do you wear blue jeans to a local formal dinner party?

I SAW YOU AT THE CONVENTION

Conventions serve a good purpose in disseminating information, inspiring its participants, providing in-service training, increasing know-how, building morale, and for learning new ideas from others. Conventions should be for all administrators and not just for the superintendents. Many administrators including classified should have their expenses paid and attend appropriate conventions. This should be accomplished by policy and not by granting favors to a chosen few. If funds do not permit all the principals or all the classified department heads to attend each year, then the policy should provide for some to attend every other year or even every third year.

Board members should be encouraged to attend conventions for board members and possibly those for superintendents. Money spent for classified department heads to attend the annual state convention for school business officials is a good investment for the district. Convention attendance is for the good of the district and not another fringe benefit granted to administrators.

This is what I like about conventions--they
INSPIRE me!

The other side of the coin is that some
who attend conventions seem to have as their
chief purpose a chance to get away from home,
to get drunk, or to play poker with old pals.
A convention is the last place to go "to kick
up your heels." It can ruin your future and
hurt your district. We can give names, dates,
and places of good administrators who were
irreparably hurt professionally by misconduct
at conferences.

The board, staff, and community should
know as far as your district is concerned,
conventions (conferences is a better term)
are a matter of serious business.

SOCIAL EVENTS

It is better for you as a school administrator for no one to remember you were at a
social event than for everyone to remember you
were there. This is true because you are
probably not important enough for everyone to
notice and remember you and if they do, then
it means you are dancing on the table with a
lamp shade on your head or some other ridiculous
act.

Please don't construe from this that the
school administrator is supposed to be a prude
who has no fun. We hope all school administrators enjoy life, are happy and relaxed.
But we caution against being the party clown,
the buffoon, or the obnoxious extrovert.

One aspect of school connected social
events that has often caused the unwary school
administrator trouble is food. Never be the
least bit critical of the dishes prepared by

I wonder if anyone will remember I was here.

215

parents at pot luck dinners or cookies and
pastries for parties. If you don't like lemon
pie and some ends up on your plate, do your
best to enjoy it.

Have the common courtesies for social
events and practice them. Have fun and enjoy
yourself but don't overdo the drinking and
carousing.

DON'T DANCE ON YOUR OWN TABLE

This old American Indian saying of "Don't
dance on your own table" was restated in early
days as, "Don't dip your quill in the company
inkwell." The modernized version is, "Don't
get your honey where you get your money."

When an administrator violates this wise
adage he soon faces all sorts of human and
personal problems. Jealousy, charges of
favoritism, job neglect, and absenteeism are
but a few. It is far less complicated to keep
one's business and love life separated.

This is sometimes difficult. After all,
you spend one-half of your waking life with
the people at work. You must get to know a
person well and have great trust before sharing
your love life. You can gain that knowledge
and faith in those with whom you work.

But when the accounting comes, and it
always does, the boss will probably repeat
those familiar questions, "Why didn't you get
out of town for that? Why did you have to upset
the whole office with your antics?"   The
authors believe that even if religion is not
"your thing," you will still come out ahead

DON'T DANCE ON OWN TABLE!

to observe a high code of morality even just for selfish, professional advancement.

For school administrators in medium-sized or small communities the advice of not dancing on your own table is particularly good. An elementary principal lost his job because he was playing around with the PTA President; a business manager was fired partly because he was having an affair with the bookkeeper. You are certainly entitled to live your own life, but when those actions start interfering with the work is when problems arise. You can prevent this by not getting your honey where you get your money!

BELIEVE IN PEOPLE

Elton Mayo postulated and described the "rabble hypothesis" of management while doing the Hawthorne studies on motivation. The opposite philosophy of treating employees as rabble to be beaten and driven is a positive belief in people.

A laboratory researcher received a shipment of 100 white rats. He painted the ears of 50 of the rats a brilliant orange before showing them to his assistants.

The assistants inquired about the orange-eared rats. The researcher shrugged and said it was of no importance but he left his office door ajar as he made an imaginary telephone call to report the receipt of the 50 specially bred, highly intelligent white rats. The conversation was overheard by the assistants.

Men, this problem is too tough for any one of us,
so I'm asking each one of you to assist me.

Over the next few months the carefully
maintained records of the laboratory proved
that the rats with orange ears learned the
mazes more rapidly, made fewer errors, and
generally out performed the "ordinary" rats.
There was no explanation--other than the
orange-eared rats were _expected_ to do better.

As an administrator you need to have
faith in those with whom you work. Faith
that they want to succeed--do a good job;
faith that they can work without constant,
degrading supervision; that they can be self-
motivated; that they will strive to perform
to your expectations.

Every person needs a chance to develop
on his own, to be creative, to be better than
he is. You can help your co-workers by having
and exercising a belief in people.

— — —

_The greatest fault of all is to have
faults and not try to correct them._

220

BIBLIOGRAPHY

221

BIBLIOGRAPHY

American Association of School Administrators.
Sex equality in educational administration.
Arlington, Virginia: AASA, 1975.

Bell, C., & French, W. Organization development:
Behavioral science interventions for organiza-
tion improvement. Salt Lake City, Utah:
Prentice Hall, 1973. (Excellent overview)

Bennis, W. G. Organization development: Its
nature, origins, and prospects. Reading,
Mass.: Addison-Wesley, 1969. (Good
overview)

Browder, L. H., Jr., Atkins, W. A., Jr., &
Kaya, E. Developing an educationally
accountable program. Berkeley, California:
McCutchan Publishing Corp., 1973.

Drucker, P. F. Management: Tasks, responsibilities & practices. New York: Harper & Row,
1973.

Filley, A. C., & House, R. H. Managerial pro-
cess and organizational behavior (2nd ed.).
Glenview, Illinois: Scott, Foresman and
Co., 197ɔ.

Gardner, J. W. Self-renewal: The individual and
the innovative society. New York: Harper
and Row, 1971.

Harrison, E. F. The managerial decision-making
process. Boston, Mass.: Houghton Mifflin
Co., 1975.

Hampton, D. R., Summer, C. E., & Webber, R. A.
Organizational behavior and the practice of
management (Rev.). Glenview, Illinois:
Scott, Foresman and Co., 1973.

Kast, F. E., & Rosenzweig, J. E. Organization
and management: A systems approach. New
York: McGraw-Hill, 1974.

Katz, D., & Kahn, R. L. The social psychology
of organizations. New York: Wiley, 1966.

Knezevich, S. J. Administration of public
education (3rd ed.). New York: Harper &
Row, 1975.

Likert, R. The human organization: Its management and value. New York: McGraw-Hill,

McGregor, D. The professional manager. New
York: McGraw-Hill, 1967.

Nierenberg, G. I. Fundamentals of negotiating.
New York: Hawthorn Books, Inc., 1973.

Odiorne, G. S. Management and the activity trap.
New York: Harper and Row, 1974.

Owens, R. G., & Steinhoff, C. R. Administering
change in schools. Englewood Cliffs, New
Jersey: Prentice-Hall, Inc., 1976.

Raia, A. P. Managing by objectives. Glenview,
Illinois: Scott, Foresman and Company, 1974.

Reddin, W. J. Effective management by objectives:
The 3-D method of MBO. New York: McGraw-
Hill, 1971.

Sergiovanni, T., & Carver, F. D. The new school
executive: A theory of administration. New
York: Dodd, Mead & Co., 1973.
223

Saxe, R. W. School community interaction.
    Berkeley, California: McCutchan
    Publishing, 1975.

Vroom, V. H., & Yetton, P. W. Leadership and
    decision making. Pittsburgh: University of
    Pittsburgh Press, 1973.